بسم الله الرحمن الرحيم

# ABOUT THE AUTHOR

Under the pen-name HARUN YAHYA, the author has published many books on political and faith-related issues. An important body of his work deals with the materialistic world view and the impact of it in world history and politics. (The pen-name is formed from the names 'Harun' [Aaron] and 'Yahya' [John] in the esteemed memory of the two Prophets who struggled against infidelity.)

His works include *Judaism and Freemasonry, Freemasonry and Capitalism, Satan's Religion: Freemasonry, Jehovah's Sons and the Freemasons, The New Masonic Order, The 'Secret Hand' in Bosnia, The Holocaust Hoax, Behind the Scenes of Terrorism, Israel's Kurdish Card, A National Strategy for Turkey, Darwin's Antagonism Against the Turks, The Evolution Deceit, Perished Nations, For Men of Understanding, The Golden Age, The Colour Art of Allah, The Truth of the Life of This World, Confessions of Evolutionists, The Misconceptions of Evolutionists, The Qur'an Leads the Way to Science, The Design in Nature, Self-Sacrifice and Intelligent Models of Behaviour in Living Beings, Eternity Has Already Started, Kids Darwin Lied!, The End of Darwinism, The Creation of the Universe, Never Feign Ignorance, Timelessness and the Reality of Fate, The Miracle of the Atom, The Miracle in the Cell, The Miracle of the Immune System, The Miracle in the Eye, The Creation Miracle in Plants, The Miracle in the Spider, The Miracle in the Gnat, The Miracle in the Honeybee, The Miracle in the Ant.*

Among his booklets are *The Mystery of the Atom, The Collapse of the Theory of Evolution: The Fact of Creation, The Collapse of Materialism, The End of Materialism, The Blunders of Evolutionists 1, The Blunders of Evolutionists 2, The Microbiological Collapse of Evolution, The Fact of Creation, The Collapse of the Theory of Evolution in 20 Questions, The Biggest Deception in the History of Biology: Darwinism.*

The author's other works on Quranic topics include: *Ever Thought About the Truth?, Devoted to Allah, Abandoning the Society of Ignorance, Paradise, The Theory of Evolution, Moral Values in the Qur'an, Knowledge of the Qur'an, Qur'an Index, Emigrating for the Cause of Allah, The Character of Hypocrites in the Qur'an, The Secrets of the Hypocrite, The Epithets of Allah, Communicating the Message and Disputing in the Qur'an, Basic Concepts in the Qur'an, Answers from the Qur'an, Death Resurrection Hell, The Struggle of the Messengers, The Avowed Enemy of Man: Satan, Idolatry, The Religion of the Ignorant, The Arrogance of Satan, Prayer in the Qur'an, The Importance of Conscience in the Qur'an, Day of Resurrection, Never Forget, Disregarded Judgements of the Qur'an, Human Characters in the Society of Ignorance, The Importance of Patience in the Qur'an, General Knowledge from the Qur'an, Quick Grasp of Faith 1-2-3, The Crude Reasoning of Disbelief, Perfected Faith, Before Regretting, Our Messengers Say, The Compassion of Believers, Fear of Allah, The Nightmare of Disbelief, Prophet Isa Will Come, Beauties Presented to Life by the Qur'an, A Collection from Allah's Beauties 1-2-3*

# ALLAH IS KNOWN THROUGH REASON

# ALLAH IS KNOWN THROUGH REASON

HARUN YAHYA

*Goodword*
B·O·O·K·S

First published 2000
Reprinted 2002, 2003, 2005, 2008
© Goodword Books 2008

Goodword Books
1, Nizamuddin West Market
New Delhi - 110 013
email: info@goodwordbooks.com
Printed in India

www.goodwordbooks.com

# CONTENTS

## PART I
## THE FACT OF CREATION
## IN THE LIGHT OF SCIENTIFIC EVIDENCE

Introduction 10
From Non-Being to Being 14
The Signs in the Heavens and on the Earth 30
Scientists Confirm the Signs of Allah 64
Scientific Facts and the Miracle of the Qur'an 70

## PART II
## THOSE WHO ARE UNABLE TO SEE THE FACT OF CREATION

Evolution Deceit 100
Philosophies that made the Mistake of Denying Allah 131
The Harms of a Society Model with No Belief in Allah 139
The True Promised Home: The Hereafter 144
A Very Different Approach to Matter 156
Relativity of Time and the Reality of Fate 192
Conclusion 204
Footnotes 208

# PART I

# THE FACT OF CREATION

## IN THE LIGHT OF SCIENTIFIC EVIDENCE

# Introduction

Take a look around you from where you sit. You will notice that everything in the room is 'made': the walls, the upholstery, the ceiling, the chair where you sit, the book you hold in your hand, the glass on the table and countless other details. None of them happen to exist in your room of their own accord. Even the simple loops of the carpet were made by someone: they did not appear spontaneously or by chance.

A person who is about to read a book knows that it has been written by an author for a specific reason. It would not even occur to him that this book might have come into being by chance. In the same manner, a person who sees a sculpture has no doubt whatsoever that it was made by a sculptor. And not just works of art: even a few bricks resting on top of one another make one think that they must have been brought to rest just so by someone within a certain plan. Therefore, everywhere where there is an order – either small or big – a founder and protector of this order must also exist. If, one day, somebody came forward and said that raw iron and coal came together to form steel by chance, which in turn constructed the Eiffel Tower again by chance, would not he and those who believed him be regarded as insane?

The claim of the theory of evolution, the unique method of denying the existence of Allah, is no different than this. According to the theory, inorganic molecules formed amino acids by chance, amino acids formed proteins by chance, and finally proteins formed living creatures again by chance. However, the probability of a living creature being formed by coincidence is less than the probability of the Eiffel Tower being formed in the same manner, because even the simplest human cell is more sophisticated than any man-made structure in the world.

How is it possible to think that the balance in the world came about by coincidence when the extraordinary harmony of nature is observable even with the naked eye? It is the most unreasonable claim to say that the universe, each point of which suggests the existence of its Creator, has come into being on its own.

Therefore, there should be an owner of the balance visible everywhere from our body to the farthest corners of the inconceivably vast universe. So, who is this Creator that ordained everything so subtly and created all?

He cannot be any material being present within the universe, because His must be a will that existed before the universe and created the universe thereupon. The Almighty Creator is One Whom everything finds existence, yet Whose existence is without any beginning or end.

Religion teaches us the identity of our Creator Whose existence we discover with our reason. Through what He has revealed to us as religion, we know that He is Allah, the Compassionate and the Merciful, Who created the heavens and the earth from nothing.

Although most people have the capability to grasp this fact, they spend their lives unaware of it. When they look at a landscape painting, they wonder who its painter is. Later, they praise the artist at length for his beautiful work of art. Despite the fact that they face numerous originals of that painting the moment they turn around, they still disregard the existence of Allah, Who is the only owner of all these beauties. In truth, not even a lengthy research is needed to understand the existence of Allah. Even if one had to live in a room from the time he was born, countless pieces of evidence in this room alone would be enough for him to grasp the existence of Allah.

The human body so overflows with evidence that it could not be contained in many multi-volumed encyclopaedias. Even giving a few minutes of conscientious thought to it all is enough to understand the existence of Allah. The present order is protected by Allah and maintained by Him.

The human body is not the only food for thought. Life abides in every square millimetre of the earth, be it observable by men or not. The world overflows with many living beings, from unicellular organisms to plants, from insects to sea animals, and from birds to human beings. If you take a handful of soil and look at it, even therein you can discover manifold living creatures with diverse characteristics. The same is true also for the air you breathe. Even on your skin, there are many living creatures whose names are unknown to you. In the intestines of all living beings are millions of bacteria or unicellular organisms that help digestion. The animal population in the world is many times greater than the human population. When we also consider the plant world, we see that there is not a single spot on the earth where there is no life. All of these creatures that are spread over an area of millions of square kilometres have different body systems, different lives and different contributions to the ecological balance. It is preposterous to claim that all these have come into existence by chance with no aim or purpose. No living being has come to exist through its own accord or effort. No coincidental happening can ever result in such complicated systems.

All of this evidence leads us to the conclusion that the universe works with a certain 'consciousness'. What, then, is the source of this consciousness? Surely it is neither the living nor the non-living beings in it. Nor can they be the ones that maintain the harmony and preserve the order. The existence and glory of Allah reveals itself in countless proofs in the universe. In fact, there is not even a single man on the earth who will not accept this evident reality from the heart. Yet they still deny it 'in iniquity and arrogance though their souls are convinced thereof' as stated in the Qur'an. (Surat an-Naml, 14)

This book is written to point out this reality from which some people turn away because of its being at odds with their interests, and also to disclose the frauds and senseless deductions on which some untrue allegations stand. This is why many diverse subjects are tackled in the book.

Those who read this book will once more see the indisputable evidence of Allah's existence and witness that Allah's existence encompasses all things: the 'reason' knows this. Just as He has created this all-pervading order, He is the One Who also maintains it incessantly.

# From Non - Being to Being

The questions of how the universe originated, where it leads to, and how the laws maintaining its order and balance work have always been topics of interest. Scientists and thinkers have thought about this subject endlessly and have produced quite a few theories.

The prevailing thought until the early 20th century was that the universe had infinite dimensions, that it had existed since eternity, and that it would continue to exist forever. According to this view, called the 'static universe model', the universe had neither a beginning nor an end.

Laying the groundwork for the materialist philosophy, this view denied the existence of a Creator while it maintained that the universe is a constant, stable, and unchanging collection of matter.

Materialism is a system of thought that holds matter to be an absolute being and denies the existence of anything but matter. Having its roots in ancient Greece and gaining ever-increasing acceptance in the 19th century, this system of thought became famous in the shape of the dialectical materialism of Karl Marx.

As we have stated earlier, the static universe model of the 19th century prepared the grounds for the materialist philosophy. In his book *Principes Fondamentaux de Philosophie,* George Politzer stated concerning the basis of this universe model that "the universe was not a created object", and added:

If it were, then it would have to be created instantaneously by God and brought into existence from nothing. To admit creation, one has to admit, in the first place, the existence of a moment when the universe did not exist, and that something came out of nothingness. This is something to which science cannot accede.[1]

When Politzer asserted that the universe was not created out of nothingness, he was relying on the static universe model of the 19th century, and thinking that he was posing a scientific claim. However, the 20th century's developing science and technology demolished primitive concepts such as the static universe model that laid the grounds for the materialists. Today, on the brink of the 21st century, modern physics has proved with many experiments, observations and calculations that the universe had a beginning and that it was created out of nothing with a big explosion.

That the universe had a beginning means that the cosmos was brought into being out of nothing, that is, that it was created. If a created thing exists (which did not exist beforehand), then it certainly should have a Creator. Being from non-being is something inconceivable by the human mind. (Man cannot practically conceive it since he has no chance of experiencing it.) Therefore, being from non-being is very different from bringing objects together to form a new object (such as works of art or technological inventions). It is a sign of Allah's creation alone that everything formed perfectly all at once and in a single moment, when the created things had no previous examples and not even time and space existed in which to create them.

The coming of the universe into being from non-being is the greatest proof possible that it has been created. Consideration of this fact will change a lot of things. It helps people understand the meaning of life and review their attitudes and purposes. This is why many scientific communities have tried to disregard the fact of creation which they could not fully comprehend, even though its evidence was clear to them. The fact that all scientific evidence points to the existence of a Creator has compelled them to invent alternatives to create confusion in the minds of people. Nevertheless, the evidence of science itself puts a definite end to these theories.

Now, let us take a brief look at the scientific developmental process through which the universe came about.

## THE EXPANSION OF THE UNIVERSE

In 1929, in the California Mount Wilson observatory, an American astronomer by the name of Edwin Hubble made one of the greatest discoveries in the history of astronomy. While he observed the stars with a giant telescope, he found out that the light from them was shifted to the red end of the spectrum and that this shift was more pronounced the further a star was from the earth. This discovery had an electrifying effect in the world of science, because according to the recognised rules of physics, the spectra of light beams travelling towards the point of observation tend towards violet while the spectra of the light beams moving away from the point of observation tend towards red. During Hubble's observations, the light from stars was discovered to tend towards red. This meant that they were constantly moving away from us.

Before long, Hubble made another very important discovery: Stars and galaxies moved away not only from us, but also from one another. The only conclusion that could be derived from a universe where everything moves away from everything else is that the universe constantly 'expands'.

To better understand, the universe can be thought of as the surface of a balloon being blown up. Just as the points on the surface of a balloon move apart from each other as the balloon is inflated, so do the objects in space move apart from each other as the universe keeps expanding.

In fact, this had been theoretically discovered even earlier. Albert Einstein, who is considered the greatest scientist of the century, had concluded after the calculations he made in theoretical physics that the universe could not be static. However, he had laid his discovery to rest simply not to conflict with the widely recognised static universe model of his time. Later on, Einstein was to identify his act as 'the greatest mistake of his career'. Subsequently, it became definite by Hubble's observations that the universe expands.

What importance, then, did the fact that the universe expands have on the existence of the universe?

The expansion of the universe implied that if it could travel backwards in time, the universe would prove to have originated from a single

**Edwin Hubble, next to his giant telescope.**

point. The calculations showed that this 'single point' that harboured all the matter of the universe should have 'zero volume' and 'infinite density'. The universe had come about by the explosion of this single point with zero volume. This great explosion that marked the beginning of the universe was named the 'Big Bang' and the theory started to be so called.

It has to be stated that 'zero volume' is a theoretical expression used for descriptive purposes. Science can define the concept of 'nothingness', which is beyond the limits of human comprehension, only by expressing it as 'a point with zero volume'. In truth, 'a point with no volume' means 'nothingness'. The universe has come into being from nothingness. In other words, it was created.

The Big Bang theory showed that in the beginning all the objects in

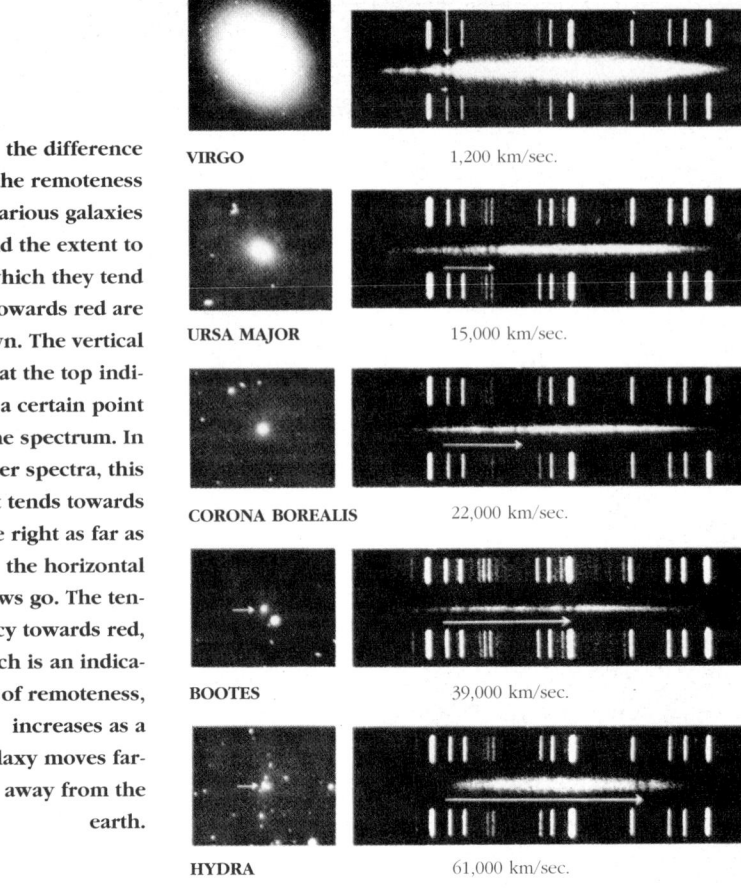

Here, the difference in the remoteness of various galaxies and the extent to which they tend towards red are shown. The vertical line at the top indicates a certain point on the spectrum. In other spectra, this point tends towards the right as far as the horizontal arrows go. The tendency towards red, which is an indication of remoteness, increases as a galaxy moves farther away from the earth.

the universe were of one piece and then were parted. This fact, which was revealed by the Big Bang theory was stated in the Qur'an 14 centuries ago, when people had a very limited knowledge about the universe:

> Do not the Unbelievers see that the heavens and the earth were joined together (as one unit of creation), before We clove them asunder? We made from water every living thing. Will they not then believe? (Surat al-Anbiya, 30)

As stated in the verse, everything, even the 'heavens and the earth' that were not yet created, were created with a Big Bang out of a single point, and shaped the present universe by being parted from each other.

When we compare the statements in the verse with the Big Bang theory, we see that they fully agree with each other. However, the Big Bang was introduced as a scientific theory only in the 20th century.

The expansion of the universe is one of the most important pieces of

Research has shown that stars and galaxies move away both from us and from one another, that is, the universe expands. This suggests that when moved backwards in time, the universe proves to have started from a single point.

*From Non-Being to Being*

evidence that the universe was created out of nothing. Although this fact was not discovered by science until the 20th century, Allah has informed us of this reality in the Qur'an revealed 1,400 years ago:

> It is We who have built the universe with (Our creative) power, and, verily, it is We who are steadily expanding it. (Surat adh-Dhariyat, 47)

## THE SEARCH FOR ALTERNATIVES TO THE BIG BANG THEORY

As clearly seen, the Big Bang theory proved that the universe was 'created from nothing', in other words, that it was created by Allah. For this reason, astronomers committed to the materialist philosophy continued to resist the Big Bang and uphold the steady-state theory. The reason for this effort was revealed in the following words of A. S. Eddington, one of the foremost materialist physicists: 'Philosophically, the notion of an abrupt beginning to the present order of Nature is repugnant to me.'[2]

Sir Fred Hoyle was one of those who were disturbed by the Big Bang theory. In the middle of the century, Hoyle championed a theory called the steady-state which was similar to the 'constant universe' approach of the 19th century. The steady-state theory argued that the universe was both infinite in size and eternal in duration. With the sole visible aim of supporting the materialist philosophy, this theory was totally at variance with the 'Big Bang' theory, which held that the universe had a beginning.

Those who defended the steady-state theory opposed the Big Bang for a long time. Science, however, was working against them.

Some scientists, on the other hand, looked for ways to develop alternatives.

In 1948, George Gamov came up with another idea concerning the Big Bang. He stated that after the formation of the universe by a big explosion, a radiation surplus should have existed in the universe left over from this explosion. Moreover, this radiation ought to be uniformly diffused across the universe

This evidence which 'ought to have existed' was soon to be found.

# MORE EVIDENCE: COSMIC BACKGROUND RADIATION

In 1965, two researchers by the name of Arno Penzias and Robert Wilson discovered these waves by chance. This radiation, called the 'cosmic background radiation', did not seem to radiate from a particular source but rather pervaded the whole of space. Thus, it was understood that the heat waves that were radiated uniformly from all around space were left over from the initial stages of the Big Bang. Penzias and Wilson were awarded a Nobel Prize for their discovery.

In 1989, NASA sent the Cosmic Background Explorer (COBE) satellite into space to do research on cosmic background radiation. It took only eight minutes for the sensitive scanners on this satellite to confirm the measurements of Penzias and Wilson. The COBE had found the remains of the big explosion that had taken place at the outset of the universe.

Defined as the greatest astronomic discovery of all times, this finding explicitly proved the Big Bang theory. The findings of the COBE 2 satellite which was sent into space after the COBE satellite also confirmed the calculations based on the Big Bang.

Another important piece of evidence for the Big Bang was the amount of hydrogen and helium in space. In the latest calculations, it was understood that the hydrogen-helium concentration in the universe complied with the theoretical calculations of the hydrogen-helium concentration remaining from the Big Bang. If the universe had no beginning and if it had existed since eternity, its hydrogen constituent should have been completely consumed and converted to helium.

All of this compelling evidence caused the Big Bang theory to be embraced by the scientific community. The Big Bang model was the latest point reached by science concerning the formation and beginning of the universe.

Defending the steady-state theory alongside Fred Hoyle for years, Dennis Sciama described the final position they had reached after all the evidence for the Big Bang theory was revealed. Sciama stated that he had taken part in the heated debate between the defenders of the steady-state

theory and those who tested that theory with the hope of refuting it. He added that he had defended the steady-state theory, not because he deemed it valid, but because he wished that it were valid. Fred Hoyle stood out against all objections as evidence against this theory began to unfold. Sciama goes on to say that he had first taken a stand along with Hoyle but, as evidence began to pile up, he had to admit that the game was over and that the steady-state theory had to be dismissed.[3]

Prof. George Abel from the University of California also states that currently available evidence shows that the universe originated billions of years ago with the Big Bang. He concedes that he has no choice but to accept the Big Bang theory.

With the Big Bang's victory, the concept of 'eternal matter' that constituted the basis of the materialist philosophy is thrown into the trash-heap of history. What, then, was before the Big Bang and what was the power that brought the universe into 'being' with this big explosion when it was 'non-existent'? This question certainly implies, in Arthur Eddington's words,

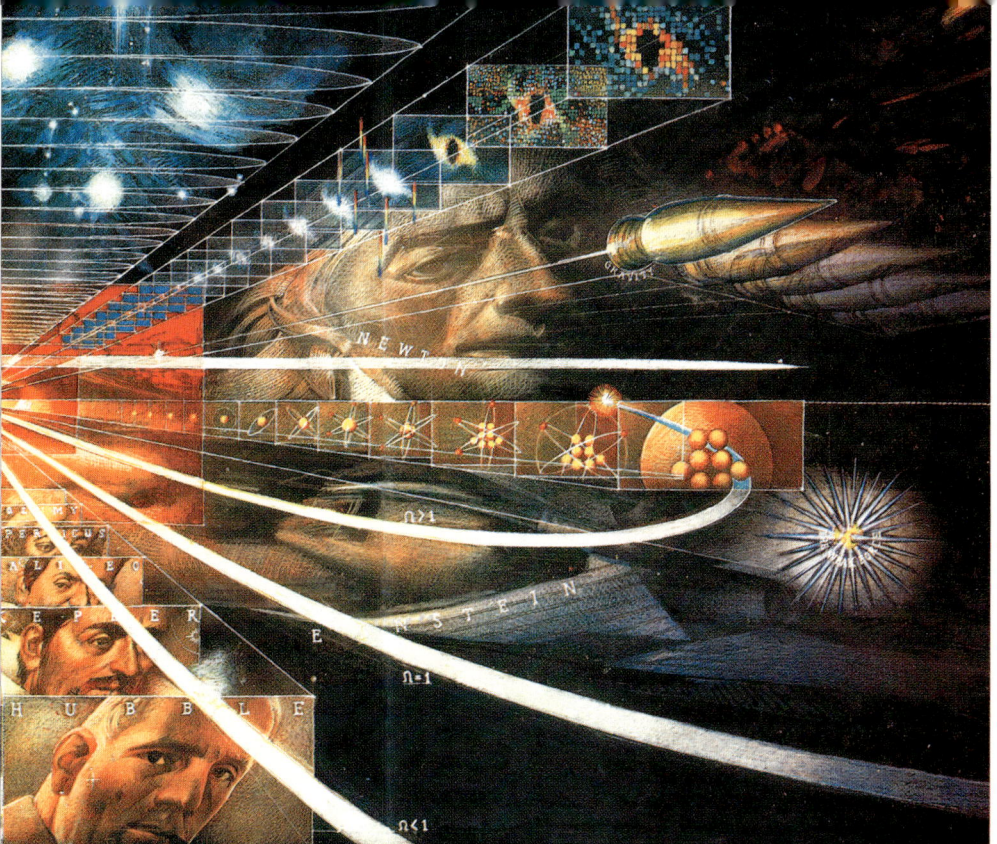

the 'philosophically unfavourable' fact for the materialists, that is, the existence of a Creator. The renowned atheist philosopher Antony Flew comments on the issue:

> Notoriously, confession is good for the soul. I will therefore begin by confessing that the Stratonician atheist has to be embarrassed by the contemporary cosmological consensus. For it seems that the cosmologists are providing a scientific proof of what St. Thomas contended could not be proved philosophically; namely, that the universe had a beginning. So long as the universe can be comfortably thought of as being not only without end but also without beginning, it remains easy to urge that its brute existence, and whatever are found to be its most fundamental features, should be accepted as the explanatory ultimates. Although I believe that it remains still correct, it certainly is neither easy nor comfortable to maintain this position in the face of the Big Bang story.[4]

Many scientists who do not blindly condition themselves to be atheists have admitted the role of an almighty Creator in the creation of the universe. This Creator must be a being Who has created both matter and time, yet Who is independent of both. Well-known astrophysicist Hugh Ross has this to say:

> If time's beginning is concurrent with the beginning of the universe, as the space-theorem says, then the cause of the universe must be some entity operating in a time dimension completely independent of and pre-existent to the time dimension of the cosmos. This conclusion is powerfully important to our understanding of who God is and who or what God isn't. It tells us that God is not the universe itself, nor is God contained within the universe.[5]

Matter and time are created by the almighty Creator Who is independent of all these notions. This Creator is Allah, Who is the Lord of the heavens and the earth.

## DELICATE BALANCES IN SPACE

In truth, the Big Bang caused much greater trouble for the materialists than the above confessions of the atheist philosopher, Antony Flew. For the Big Bang not only proves that the universe was created out of nothing, but also that it was brought into being in a very planned, systematic and controlled manner.

The Big Bang took place with the explosion of the point which contained all the matter and energy of the universe and its dispersion into space in all directions with a terrifying speed. Out of this matter and energy, there came about a great balance containing galaxies, stars, the sun, the earth and all other heavenly bodies. Moreover, laws were formed called the 'laws of physics', which are uniform throughout the whole universe and do not change. All these indicate that a perfect order arose after the Big Bang.

Explosions, however, do not bring about order. All of the observable explosions tend to harm, disintegrate, and destroy what is present. For example, the atom and hydrogen bomb explosions, fire-damp explosions, volcanic explosions, natural gas explosions, solar explosions: they all have destructive effects.

If we were to be introduced to a very detailed order after an explosion - for instance, if an explosion under the ground gave rise to perfect works of art, huge palaces, or imposing houses - we might conclude that there was a 'supernatural' intervention behind this explosion and that all the pieces dispersed by the explosion had been made to move in a very controlled way.

The quote from Sir Fred Hoyle, who accepted his mistake after many years of opposition to the Big Bang Theory, expresses this situation very well:

> The big bang theory holds that the universe began with a single explosion. Yet as can be seen below, an explosion merely throws matter apart, while the big bang has mysteriously produced the opposite effect - with matter clumping together in the form of galaxies.[6]

While stating that the Big Bang's giving way to order is contradictory, he surely interprets the Big Bang with a materialistic bias and assumes that this was an 'uncontrolled explosion'. He, however, was in reality the one who became self-contradictory by making such a statement simply to dismiss the existence of a Creator. For if a great order arose with an explosion, then the concept of an 'uncontrolled explosion' should have been set aside and it should be accepted that the explosion was extraordinarily controlled.

Another aspect of this extraordinary order formed in the universe following the Big Bang is the creation of a 'habitable universe'. The conditions for the formation of a habitable planet are so many and so complex that it is almost impossible to think that this formation is coincidental.

Paul Davies, a renowned professor of theoretical physics, calculated how 'fine tuned' the pace of expansion after the Big Bang was, and he reached an incredible conclusion. According to Davies, if the rate of expansion after the Big Bang had been different even by the ratio of one over a billion times a billion, no habitable star type would have been formed:

> Careful measurement puts the rate of expansion very close to a critical value at which the universe will just escape its own gravity and expand

*From Non-Being to Being*

forever. A little slower and the cosmos would collapse, a little faster and the cosmic material would have long ago completely dispersed. It is interesting to ask precisely how delicately the rate of expansion has been 'fine-tuned' to fall on this narrow dividing line between two catastrophes. If at time I S (by which time the pattern of expansion was already firmly established) the expansion rate had differed from its actual value by more than 10-18, it would have been sufficient to throw the delicate balance out. The explosive vigour of the universe is thus matched with almost unbelievable accuracy to its gravitating power. The big bang was not, evidently, any old bang, but an explosion of exquisitely arranged magnitude.[7]

The laws of physics that emerged together with the Big Bang did not change at all over a period of 15 billion years. Furthermore, these laws stand on calculations so scrupulous that even a millimetre's variation from their current values can result in the destruction of the whole structure and configuration of the universe.

The famous physicist Prof. Stephen Hawking states in his book *A Brief History of Time*, that the universe is set on calculations and balances more finely tuned than we can conceive. Hawking states with reference to the rate of expansion of the universe:

> Why did the universe start out with so nearly the critical rate of expansion that separates models that recollapse from those that go on expanding forever, so that even now, ten thousand million years later, it is still expanding at nearly the critical rate? If the rate of expansion one second after the big bang had been smaller by even one part in a hundred thousand million million, the universe would have recollapsed before it ever reached its present size.[8]

Paul Davies also explains the unavoidable consequence to be derived from these incredibly precise balances and calculations:

> It is hard to resist the impression that the present structure of the universe, apparently so sensitive to minor alterations in the numbers, has been rather carefully thought out... The seemingly miraculous concurrence of numerical values that nature has assigned to her fundamental constants must remain the most compelling evidence for an element of cosmic design.[9]

In relation to the same fact, an American professor of Astronomy, George Greenstein, writes in his book *The Symbiotic Universe:*

> As we survey all the evidence, the thought insistently arises that some supernatural agency – or, rather Agency – must be involved.[10]

## THE CREATION OF MATTER

The atom, the building-block of matter, came into being after the Big Bang. These atoms then came together to make up the universe with its stars, earth and sun. Afterwards, the same atoms established life on the earth. Everything you see around you: your body, the chair you sit on, the book you hold in your hand, the sky seen through the window, the soil, the concrete, the fruits, the plants, all living things and everything that you can imagine have come to life with the gathering of atoms.

What then is the atom, the building block of everything, made of and what kind of a structure does it have?

When we examine the structure of atoms, we see that all of them have an outstanding design and order. Every atom has a nucleus in which there are certain numbers of protons and neutrons. In addition to these, there are electrons which move around the nucleus in a constant orbit with a speed of 1,000 kms per second.[11] Electrons and protons of an atom are equal in number, because positively charged protons and negatively charged electrons always balance each other. If one of these numbers were different, there would be no atom, since its electromagnetic balance would be disturbed. An atom's nucleus, the protons and the neutrons in it, and the electrons around it are always in motion. These revolve both around themselves and each other unerringly at certain speeds. Those speeds are always proportionate to each other and provide the subsistence of the atom. No disorder, disparity, or change ever occurs.

It is very remarkable that such highly ordered and determined entities could come into being after a great explosion that took place in non-being. If the Big Bang were an uncontrolled, coincidental explosion, then it ought to have been followed by random events and everything that formed subsequently ought to have been dispersed in a great chaos.

In fact, a flawless order has prevailed at every point since the beginning of existence. For example, although atoms are formed at different places and times, they are so organised that they seem as though they were produced from a single factory with an awareness of each kind. First, electrons find themselves a nucleus and start to turn around it. Later, atoms come together to form matter and all these bring about meaningful, purposeful and reasonable objects. Ambiguous, useless, abnormal and purposeless things never occur. Everything from the smallest unit to the biggest component is organised and has manifold purposes.

All of this is solid evidence of the existence of the Creator, Who is exalted in power, and indicate the fact that everything comes into existence however He wants and whenever He wills. In the Qur'an, Allah refers to His creation thus:

> He it is Who has created the heavens and the earth with truth, and on the day He says: Be, it is. His word is the truth. (Surat al-An'am, 73)

## AFTER THE BIG BANG

As Roger Penrose, a physicist who has done extensive research on the origin of the universe, has stated the fact that the universe rests where it is not by mere coincidence shows that it definitely has a purpose. For some people, 'the universe is just there' and it just goes on being there. We just happened to find ourselves right in the middle of this whole thing. This viewpoint would probably not help us in understanding the universe. According to Penrose's view, there are many deep affairs going on within the universe whose existence we cannot today perceive.[12]

The ideas of Roger Penrose are indeed good food for thought. As these words imply, many people wrongly entertain thoughts that the universe with all its perfect harmony exists for nothing and that they live in this universe again for idle play.

However, it can by no means be considered as ordinary that a quite perfect and wondrous order came about after the Big Bang, which is considered by the scientific community to be the means of the formation of the universe.

The order in the structure of the atom rules the whole universe. With the atom and its particles moving in a certain order, the mountains are not scattered, lands do not break apart, the sky is not split asunder and, in short, matter is held together and is constant.

Briefly, when we examine the glorious system in the universe, we see that the existence of the universe and its workings rest on extremely delicate balances and an order too complex to be explained away by coincidental causes. As is evident, it is by no means possible for this delicate balance and order to have been formed on its own and by coincidence after a great explosion. The formation of such an order following an explosion such as the Big Bang could only have been possible as a result of a supernatural creation.

This matchless plan and order in the universe certainly proves the existence of a Creator with infinite knowledge, might and wisdom, Who has created matter from nothing and Who controls and manages it incessantly. This Creator is Allah, the Lord of the heavens, the earth and all that is in between.

All these facts also show us how the claims of the materialist philosophy, which is simply a 19th century dogma, are invalidated by 20th century science.

By exposing the great plan, design and order prevalent in the universe, modern science has proved the existence of a Creator Who has created and rules all beings: that is, Allah.

Holding sway over a great number of people for centuries and having even disguised itself with the mask of 'science', materialism, by deeming everything to consist of nothing but matter, has made a great mistake and denied the existence of Allah, Who created and ordered matter from nothing. One day, materialism will be remembered in history as a primitive and superstitious belief opposing both reason and science.

*From Non-Being to Being*

# The Signs in the Heavens and on the Earth

Assume that you set up a big city by bringing millions of Legos together. Let there be in this city skyscrapers, twisting roads, railway stations, airports, shopping malls, subways and also rivers, lakes, forests and a beach. Let there also be living in it thousands of people wandering in its streets, sitting in their homes and working in their offices. Take every detail into account. Even the traffic lights, box offices, and the signboards at the bus stations.

If someone came up to you and said that all the Legos of this city, which you had founded by planning it right down to the smallest detail, and each piece of which you had picked up with great pains, had been brought together by coincidence to produce this city, what would you think of the mental state of that person?

Now, go back to the city you have built and consider that the whole city would be levelled to the ground if you had forgotten to put into place even a single Lego, or changed its place. Can you imagine what great balance and order you have had to establish?

Life in the world where we live is also made possible by the accumulation of such a great number of details incomprehensible to the human mind. The absence of even one of these details might mean the end of life on the earth.

Everything, every detail from the atom, the smallest unit of matter, to the galaxies harbouring billions of stars, from the moon, an inseparable adjunct of the world, to the solar system, all work in a perfect harmony.

This well-organised system runs flawlessly, just like a watch. People are so confident that this billions-of-years-old system will go on functioning without leaving out even the smallest detail that they can freely make plans about something they think will be realised in the next 10 years. No one is worried about whether the sun will rise the next day. A great majority of people do not think about 'whether the world may ever chance to break free from the gravitation of the sun and start to move towards the unknown in the pitch-dark space'; or ask 'What keeps this from happening?'

In the same manner, when people are about to sleep, they are very confident that their hearts or respiratory systems will not relax as their brains do. However, even a few seconds' halt in any one of these two vital systems may well cause results that will cost one's life.

When the 'glasses of familiarity' which surround the whole of life and cause every event to be assessed as if 'it is taking place in its natural course' are taken off, one is free to see that everything is made up of such closely interdependent, meticulously planned systems that it is as if we were hanging on to life by the skin of our teeth. You notice an excellent order prevailing in every spot you turn your eyes on. Certainly, there is a great power that creates such an order and harmony. The possessor of this great power is Allah, Who created everything out of nothing. In a verse of the Qur'an, it is said:

> He Who has created seven heavens in full harmony with one another: no incongruity will you see in the creation of the Most Gracious. And turn your vision (upon it) once more: can you see any flaw? Yea, turn your vision (upon it) again and yet again: (and every time) your vision will fall back upon you, dazzled and truly defeated. (Surat al-Mulk, 3-4)

When we look at the living beings in the heavens, on the earth and in all that lies between them, we see that they all prove the existence of their Creator in their own right. In this chapter, we are going to dwell on the natural phenomena and living beings that every one sees, yet never thinks about, and how they have come into being and continue their existence. If we were to write down all the signs of Allah in the universe, they would fill many thousands of volumes of encyclopaedias. Therefore, in this chapter, we will only deal briefly with some subjects that deserve to be pondered upon at length.

However, even these brief mentions will help the conscientious 'men of understanding' to notice the most important fact of their lives or at least will help them remember it once again.

For Allah Exists.

To Him is due the primal origin of the heavens and the earth and He is known through reason.

## THE MIRACLES IN OUR BODY
### 'A Half-Developed Eye Cannot See'

What comes to your mind first when you hear the word 'eye'? Are you aware that one of the most crucial things in life for you is your ability to see? Even if you are, have you ever thought what other signs your eye bears?

The eye is one of the most manifest pieces of evidence that living creatures are created. All sight organs, including animal eyes and the human eye, are extremely striking examples of a perfect design. This exceptional organ is so overwhelmingly complex that it surpasses even the most sophisticated devices in the world.

In order for an eye to see, all of its parts have to co-exist and work in harmony. For instance, if an eye happened to have lost its eyelid, but still had all the other parts such as the cornea, conjunctiva, iris, pupil, eye lenses, retina, choroid, eye muscles, and tear glands, it would still be greatly damaged and soon lose its seeing function. In the same manner, even if all its organelles were present, if the tear production were stopped, the eye would soon dry out and become blind.

'The chain of coincidences' posited by evolutionists loses all its meaning against the complex structure of the eye. It is not possible to explain the existence of the eye other than as a matter of special creation. The eye has a multi-sectioned complex system and, as discussed above, all of these individual sections had to come into existence at the same time. It is impossible for a half-developed eye to function at 'half capacity'. In such

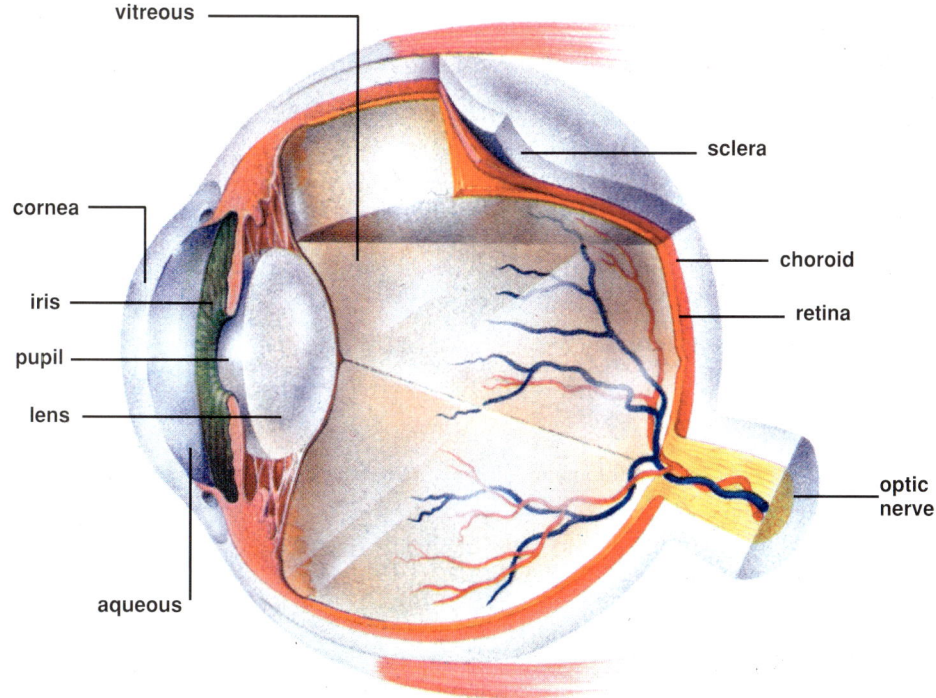

**The eye, which has an extremely complex structure, is not able to see in the absence of even a single one of its components, for instance the tear glands, when the act of seeing takes place.**

a circumstance, the act of seeing can by no means take place. An evolutionist scientist admits to this truth:

> The common trait of the eyes and the wings is that they can only function if they are fully developed. In other words, a halfway-developed eye cannot see; a bird with half-formed wings cannot fly.[13]

In this case, we again face that very important question: who created all of the components of the eye all at once?

The owner of the eyes is obviously not the one who makes the decision about their formation. For it is impossible for a being devoid of the knowledge of what seeing is like, to desire to have a seeing organ and have it attached to his body. So we have to accept the existence of a Possessor of superior Wisdom Who has created living beings with senses such as seeing, hearing, and so on. Another claim is that unconscious cells gained consciousness-requiring functions such as seeing and hearing by their own desire and effort. It is very clear that this is impossible. In the Qur'an, it is stated that seeing has been bestowed upon living beings by Allah:

> Say: He it is Who brought you into being and made for you the ears and the eyes and the hearts: little is it that you give thanks. (Surat al-Mulk, 23)

### The Army Inside Man

Every day, a war is fought in the innermost parts of your body unperceived by you. On the one side are viruses and bacteria that aim to intrude into your body and take it under control and on the other are the immunity cells that protect the body against these enemies.

The enemies wait in an offensive state to make their way into the area they aim at and they head towards the target area at the first opportunity. However, the strong, organised and disciplined soldiers of the target area do not easily give in to the enemies. First, the soldiers who swallow and neutralise the enemy soldiers (phagocytes) arrive at the battleground. However, sometimes the fight is tougher than these soldiers can handle. On such occasions, other soldiers (macrophages) are summoned up. Their involvement causes alarm in the target area and other soldiers (auxiliary T cells) are also called to battle.

These soldiers are very familiar with the local populace. They quickly distinguish their own army from that of the enemy. They immediately activate the soldiers assigned to weapon production (B cells). These soldiers have extraordinary abilities. Although they never see the enemy, they can produce weapons which will render the enemy ineffectual. In addition, they carry the weapons they produce as far as they should be taken. During this journey, they succeed in the difficult task of not causing any harm either to themselves or to their allies. Later, the striker teams cut in (killer T cells). These discharge the poisonous material they carry on themselves at the most vital spot of the enemy. In case of victory, another group of soldiers arrives at the battleground (oppressive T cells) and sends all the warriors back to their camp. The soldiers who arrive at the battleground

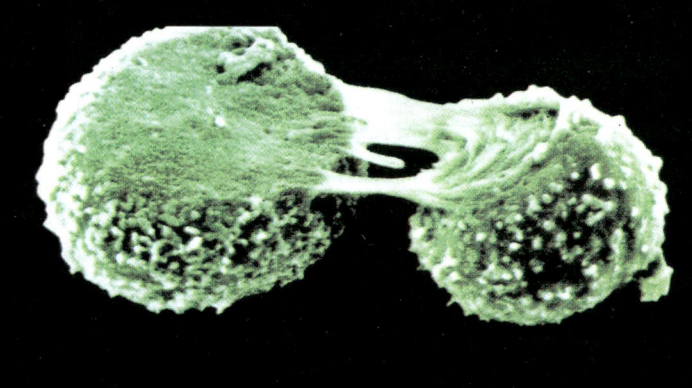

A B cell is seen as it is disjoined.

Immunity cells have an extremely disciplined command chain. None of them ever disobeys orders.

A B cell covered with bacteria.

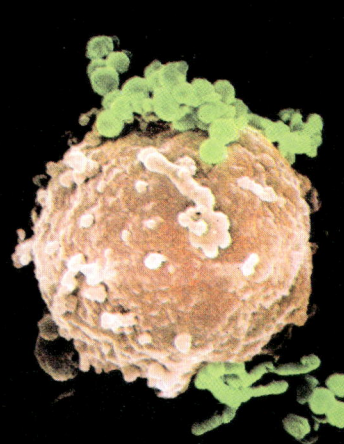

last (memory cells) record all relevant information about the enemy, so that it can be used in the event of a similar invasion in the future.

The excellent army discussed above is the immunity system in the human body. Everything explained above is done by microscopic cells unobservable to the naked eye. (For more information please see *For Men of Understanding: The Signs in the Heavens and the Earth* by Harun Yahya)

How many people are aware that they have such an organised, disciplined and perfect army inside their bodies? How many of them are aware that they are surrounded on all sides by microbes that, if unimpeded, would cause them to catch serious illnesses or even die? Indeed, there are many dangerous microbes in the air we breathe, the water we drink, the food we eat, and the surfaces we touch. While one is unaware of all that is going on, the cells in one's body make strenuous efforts to save one from an illness that may even bring about one's death.

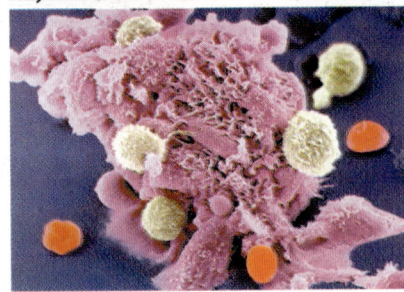

**Immunity cells (yellow) are seen in a fight with cancer cells.**

The ability of all immunity cells to distinguish enemy cells from body cells, the ability of B cells to prepare a weapon to neutralise the enemy that they have never seen, their ability to carry these weapons as far as they have to be taken without adversely affecting any body cells, the signal-receiving cells' fulfilling their duty completely without making any objections, each of them knowing what to do, their returning to their places without any problem as soon as they are finished with their work, and the abilities of the memory cells are only some of the distinctive characteristics of this system.

For all these reasons, the story of the formation of the immunity system is never taken up by any evolutionist writer.

It is extremely difficult for a person without an immunity system or with an ill-functioning one to survive, since he would be exposed to all the microbes and viruses in the outside world. Today, such people can exist only in special enclosures with no direct contact with anyone or anything outside. Therefore, it is impossible for a person without an immunity system to survive in a primitive environment. This leads us to the fact that an extremely complex system such as the immunity system could only have been created all at once and with all of its elements.

### A System Planned in its Every Detail

Breathing, eating, walking, etc, are very natural human functions. But most people do not think how these basic actions take place. For example, when you eat a fruit, you do not think how it will be made useful to your body. The only thing on your mind is eating a healthy meal; at the same time, your body is involved in extremely detailed processes unimaginable to you in order to make this meal a health-giving thing.

The digestive system where these detailed processes take place starts to function as soon as a piece of food is taken into the mouth. Being involved in the system right at the outset, the saliva wets the food and helps it to be ground by the teeth and slide down the oesophagus.

The oesophagus helps the food be transported to the stomach where a perfect balance is at work. Here, the food is digested by the hydrochloric acid present in the stomach. This acid is so strong that it has the capacity to dissolve not only the food but also the stomach walls. Of course, such a flaw is not permitted in this perfect system. A secretion called mucus which is secreted during digestion covers all the walls of the stomach and provides a perfect protection against the destructive effect of the hydrochloric acid. Thus the stomach is prevented from destroying itself.

The rest of the digestive system is likewise planned. The useful food pieces broken down by the digestive system are absorbed by the small intestine walls and enter the blood stream. The inner surface of the small intestine is covered with tiny tendrils called 'villus'. On top of the cells over the villus are microscopic extensions called the microvillus. These extensions function as pumps to absorb the nutrition. This way the nutrition absorbed by these pumps is delivered all around the body by the circulatory system.

The point that deserves attention here is that evolution can by no means explain the system briefly summarised earlier. Evolution maintains that today's complex organisms have evolved from primitive beings by the gradual accumulation of small structural changes. However, as stated clearly, the system in the stomach could in no way have been formed step by step. The absence of even one factor would bring about the death of the organism.

When food is received into the stomach, the gastric juices acquire the ability to break down food as a result of a series of chemical changes. Now, imagine a living being in the so-called evolutionary process in whose body such a planned chemical transformation is not possible. This living being, unable to acquire this ability, would not be able to digest the food it ate and would starve to death with an undigested mass of food in its stomach.

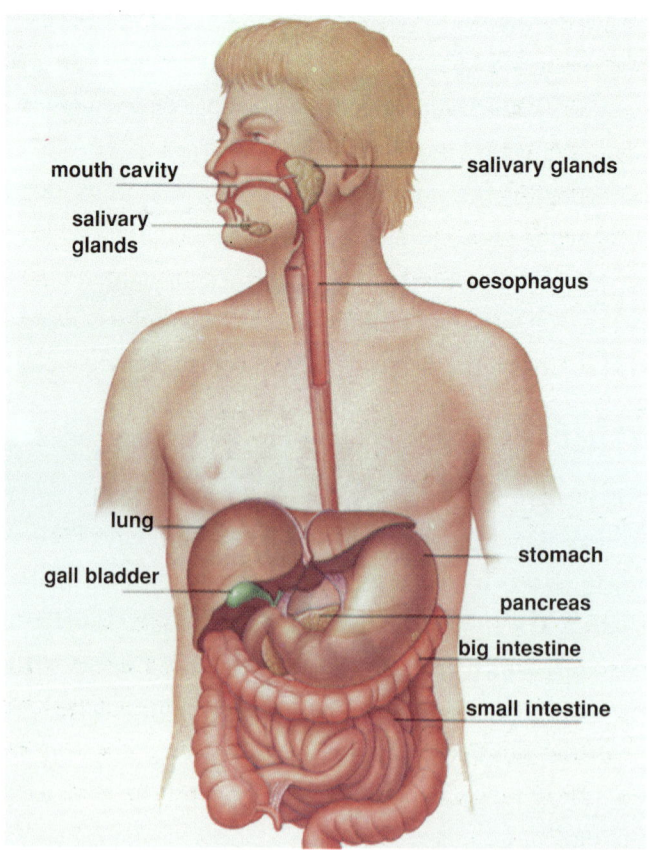

In addition, during the secretion of this dissolving acid, the stomach walls simultaneously have to produce the secretion called mucus. Otherwise, the acid in the stomach would destroy the stomach. Therefore, in order for life to continue, the stomach must secrete both fluids (acid and mucus) at the same time. This shows that not a step-by-step coincidental evolution but a conscious creation with all its systems must, in effect, have been at work.

What all this shows is that the human body resembles a huge factory made up of many small machines that work together in perfect harmony. Just as all factories have a designer, an engineer and a planner, the human body has an Exalted Creator.

## ANIMALS AND PLANTS

Millions of plant and animal types present in the world stand out as evidence that prove the existence and might of our Creator.

All of these living beings, a limited number of which will be described as examples here, deserve to be examined individually. They all have different body systems, diverse defence tactics, unique ways of feeding, and interesting reproduction methods. Unfortunately, it is not possible to describe all living beings with all their features in a single book. Encyclopaedias of many volumes would not be enough for this task.

However, even the few examples we will discuss here will be sufficient to prove that life on earth can in no way be explained by coincidences or accidental happenings.

### From Caterpillar to Butterfly

If you had 450-500 eggs and if you had to preserve them outside, what would you do? The wisest course for you would be to take precautions to prevent them from being scattered around, say, by the wind, or other environmental factors. Being one of the animals that lay the most eggs at one time (450-500), the silkworms use a very intelligent way to protect their eggs: they unite the eggs with a viscous substance (thread) they secrete to prevent them from being scattered around.

The caterpillars that pop out of their eggs firstly find a safe branch for

themselves and then get tied to this branch with the same thread. Later, to promote their own development, they start to spin a cocoon for themselves with the thread they secrete. It takes 3-4 days for a caterpillar that has opened its eyes very recently to life to complete this process. During this period, the caterpillar makes thousands of turns and produces a thread an average of 900-1,500 metres long.[14] At the end of this process, it starts a new task through which it undergoes a metamorphosis to become an elegant butterfly.

A silkworm caterpillar in its cocoon which it has spun with a silk thread.

Neither the action taken by the mother silkworm to protect its eggs, nor the behaviour of a tiny caterpillar devoid of any awareness, education or knowledge can be explained by evolution. First of all, the ability of the mother to produce the thread it uses to secure its eggs is miraculous. The newly-born caterpillar's knowing the most suitable environment for itself, its spinning a cocoon in accordance with it, its undergoing a metamorphosis, and its coming through this metamorphosis without any problem are beyond human comprehension. Hence, we can simply say that each caterpillar is born into the world with a foreknowledge of what to do, which means that it was 'taught' all of these things before it was born.

Let us explain this with an example. What would you think if you saw a new-born baby standing up a few hours after his birth, getting together the things he needs to make his bed (like quilt, pillow, mattress), and later putting all these together neatly, making his bed and lying down on it? After you recover from the shock of the event, you would probably think that the baby must have been taught in an extraordinary way in his mother's womb to perform such a process. The case of the caterpillars is no different from the baby in this example.

This again leads us to the same conclusions: these living creatures come into life, behave and live in the way determined by Allah Who has created them. The Qur'anic verse stating that Allah has inspired the honeybee and commanded it to make honey (Surat an-Nahl, 68-69) provides an example of the great secret of the world of living beings. This secret is that all living beings have bowed to Allah's will and follow the fate determined by Him. This is why the honeybee makes honey and the silkworm produces silk.

### The Symmetry in Wings

When we look at the butterfly wings in the pictures, we see a perfect symmetry prevailing over them. These lace-like wings are so adorned with patterns, spots and colours that each of them is like a work of art.

When you look at the wings of these butterflies, you notice that the patterns and colours on both sides are fully identical, no matter how intricate they may seem. Even the smallest dot is present on both wings, thereby introducing a flawless order and symmetry.

In addition, none of the colours on these thin wings mixes with the other, each being sharply set apart from the other.

The elegant and clear-cut patterns on the butterflies indicate that these living beings are not the products of unconscious coincidences but the outcomes of an excellent and matchless creation.

Actually, these colours are formed by the amassing of tiny scales clustered one on top of another. Isn't it a wonder how these small scales that are easily dispersed with your hand's slightest touch can be arranged in both wings without any mistake in their disposal so as to produce exactly the same pattern. Even the replacement of a single scale would destroy the symmetry in the wings and impair their aesthetics. However, you never see any muddle in the wings of any butterfly on the earth. They are as neat and elegant as if made by an artist. And they are indeed made by an Exalted Creator.

### The Animal with the Longest Neck: The Giraffe

Giraffes have many amazing characteristics. One of these is that their neck stands on 7 vertebrae, just like that of all other mammals, even though it is so long. Another amazing fact about giraffes is that they do not have any problem pumping blood up to their brain on top of their long

Like all other living beings, giraffes are also created with a perfect design.

44   *Allah is Known Through Reason*

neck. A little thinking would make one notice how difficult it must be to have the blood pumped so high. But giraffes do not have any problem about this, because their hearts are equipped with features to pump blood as high as necessary. This enables them to carry on with their lives effortlessly.

Yet they still face another problem while they drink water. Essentially, giraffes should have died of high blood pressure every time they bent down to drink water. However, the perfect system in their necks completely eliminates this risk. When they bend down, the valves in their neck vessels are shut down and they prevent excess blood from flowing to the brain.

> He is Allah, the Creator, the Shaper out of naught, the Bestower of forms (or colours). To Him belong the Most Beautiful Names: whatever is in the heavens and on earth, declares His Praises and Glory: and He is the Exalted in Might, the Wise.
> (Surat al-Hashr, 24)

There is no doubt that the giraffes did not acquire these traits by planning them in accordance with their needs. It is even more implausible to say that all these vital features were shaped over time through a gradual evolutionary process. In order for a giraffe to stay alive, it is vital for it to have a pumping system to transmit blood to the brain and a valve system to prevent high blood pressure the minute it bends down. If any one of these characteristics did not exist or did not function properly, then it would be impossible for the giraffe to go on living.

The conclusion to be derived from all this is that the giraffe species was born into the world with all the characteristics vital for its living. It is impossible for a non-existent being to master its body and acquire essential traits consciously. So, giraffes unquestionably prove that they are created by a conscious creation, that is by Allah.

### Sea Turtles

Sea turtles living in the oceans surge in crowds towards the beach when it is time for them to reproduce. This is no ordinary beach though. The beach they arrive at to reproduce has to be the one where they were

And in the creation of yourselves and the fact that animals are scattered (through the earth), are Signs for those of assured Faith. (Surat al-Jathiya, 4)

(Above) The young sea turtle is about to arrive at the sea before the sun rises.

born.[15] Sometimes sea turtles have to travel as far as 800 kilometres to arrive there. But a long and tough journey does not change the situation. They arrive at the beach where they were born to give birth to their offspring, no matter what.

It is quite unaccountable how a living being can find its way back to the very same beach 20-25 years after its departure from there.[16] It is all the more extraordinary that it can find the direction of its birthplace in the depths of the ocean where so little light penetrates, and then spot it from among numerous similar beaches.

Finally, thousands of travellers with no compass meet on the same beach at the same time. Initially a mystery, the reasons underlying this insistent meeting came as a great surprise when finally revealed. Since turtles know that their offspring cannot survive in sea conditions, they bury their eggs under the sand on the beach. But why do all of them meet on the same beach, at the same time? Would not the hatchlings survive if they did the same thing at different times and on different beaches? Those who did research on this topic were faced with a very interesting situation. Thousands of offspring under the sand have to overcome a number of formidable obstacles after breaking their eggs with the hard lump on their head. The hatchlings of an average of 31 grams cannot dig the earth layer above them on their own and they all help each other. When thousands of hatchlings on the beach start to dig the earth, they make it to the sand surface in a few days. Yet before they appear on the surface, they wait for a while for nightfall. For in the day time, there is the danger of falling a prey to predators. In addition, it would be quite difficult for them to proceed by crawling on sands scorched by the sunlight. When night falls, they go up to the surface after completing the digging process. Although it is dark, they rush to the sea and depart from the beach to return there as much as 20-25 years later.

It is impossible for these hatchlings to know that they have to dig their way up after they pop out of their eggs and wait for a while at a certain distance from the sea. It is by no means possible for them to know, when they are still buried in the earth, whether it is day or night, that predators

*The Signs in the Heavens and on the Earth*

exist outside and that they could fall a prey to them, that the sand is scorching because of the sun, that this could harm them, and that they must rush to the sea. So, how does this conscious conduct come about?

The only answer to this question is that these hatchlings have been somehow 'programmed' to behave in this way, which means that their Creator has inspired in them the instinct that helps them protect their lives.

**Bombardier Beetle**

The bombardier beetle is an insect on which an enormous amount of research has been done. The trait that renders this insect so popular is that it uses chemical methods to protect itself from its enemies.

In moments of danger, the insect squirts hydrogen peroxide and hydroquinone stored in its body towards the enemy to protect itself. Prior to battle, specialised structures called secretory lobes make a very concentrated mixture of these two chemicals. The mixture is stored in a separate compartment called the storage chamber. This compartment is connected to a second one called the explosion chamber. The two compartments are kept separate from one another by a sphincter muscle. The moment the insect senses danger, it squeezes the muscles surrounding the storage chamber while simultaneously relaxing the sphincter muscle, and the chemical in the storage chamber is transferred to the explosion chamber. A large quantity of heat is released and a vaporisation occurs. The released vapour and the oxygen gas exert pressure on the walls of the explo-

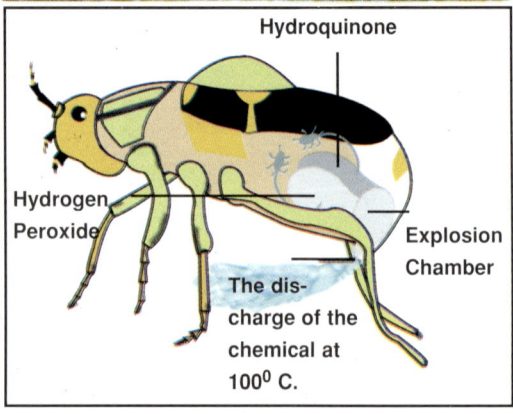

Hydroquinone

Hydrogen Peroxide

Explosion Chamber

The discharge of the chemical at $100^0$ C.

sion chamber and this chemical is squirted at the enemy through a channel leading outward from the beetle's body.[17]

It is still a great mystery to researchers how an insect can harbour inside itself a powerful system potent enough to trigger a chemical reaction that could easily cause it harm while also isolating itself from the effects of that system. No doubt, the existence and working of this system is too complicated to be attributed to the insect itself. It is still a matter of discussion how the bombardier beetle makes such a system work within its tiny body measuring about 2 cm in length, when human experts can perform it only in laboratories.

The only apparent truth here is that this insect is a concrete example completely refuting the theory of evolution, because it is impossible for this complex chemical system to have been shaped by a series of coincidental variations and passed on to future generations. Even a minor deficiency or 'defect' in a single piece of the system would leave the animal defenceless, so that it would soon be killed or it would cause it to blow itself up. Therefore, the only explanation is that the chemical weapon in the insect's body had come into being with all its parts all at once and without any defect.

**Termite Nests**

No one can help feeling surprised at the sight of a termite nest erected on the ground by termites. These nests are architectural wonders, rising as high as 5 or 6 metres.

When you compare the size of a termite and its nest, you will see that the termite has successfully completed an architectural project about 300 times bigger than itself. But what is even more astonishing is that the termites are blind.

A person who has never seen the huge nests built by blind termites would probably think that they are made up of sand piles heaped upon each other. However, a termite nest proves to be of a marvellous design incomprehensible to the human mind: inside there are intersecting tunnels, corridors, ventilation systems, special fungus production yards and safety exits.

**Being no taller than a few centimetres, termites can erect skyscrapers many metres high without using any tools. This admirable nest perfectly protects the inhabitant termite colony with a population of over a million from their enemies and unfavourable life conditions outside.**

If you assemble thousands of blind people and give them all kinds of technical tools, you can never make them set up a nest similar to the one made by the termite colony. So, just think:

- How could a termite measuring 1-2 cm. in length have learnt the architectural and engineering information needed to make such a subtle design?

- How could thousands of blind termites manage to work in harmony to build this construction which is an artistic wonder?

*Allah is Known Through Reason*

-If you divide a termite nest into two during the first stages of its construction, and then reunite it, you will see that all passage-ways, canals and roads fit each other. How can this miraculous event be explained?

The conclusion to be derived from this example is that Allah has created all living beings uniquely and without any prior example. Even one termite nest is enough for a person to comprehend Allah and believe that He is the One Who created all.

**The Woodpecker**

As we all know, woodpeckers build their nests by boring holes in tree trunks with their beaks. This may sound familiar to most people. But the point many people fail to examine is why woodpeckers suffer no brain haemorrhage when they beat a tattoo so vigorously with their heads. What the woodpecker does is in a way similar to a human being driving a nail into the wall with his head. If a man ventured to do something like that, he would probably undergo a brain shock followed by a brain haemorrhage. However, a woodpecker can peck a hard tree trunk 38-43 times in just two or three seconds and nothing happens to it.[18]

Nothing happens because the head structure of woodpeckers is ideally created for such a task. The skull of the woodpecker has a remarkable suspension system that absorbs the force of the blows. Its forehead and some skull muscles adjoined to its beak and the jaw joint are so robust that they help lessen the effect of the forceful strokes during pecking.[19]

Design and planning do not end here. Preferring primarily pine trees, woodpeckers check the age of the trees before boring a hole in them and pick those older than 100 years, because pine trees older than 100 years suffer an illness that causes the hard and thick bark to soften. This was only recently discovered by science and perhaps you

*The Signs in the Heavens and on the Earth*

may be reading of it here for the first time in your life; woodpeckers have known it for centuries.

This is not the only reason why woodpeckers prefer pine trees. Woodpeckers dig cavities around their nests, the function of which was not originally understood. These cavities were later understood to protect them from a great danger. Over time, the sticky resin that leaks from the pine trees fills up the cavities and the outpost of the woodpecker's nest is thus filled with a pool whereby woodpeckers can be protected from snakes, their greatest enemies.

Another interesting feature of woodpeckers is that their tongues are thin enough to penetrate even ants' nests in the trees. Their tongues are also sticky, which allows them to collect the ants that live there. The perfection in their creation is further revealed by the fact that their tongues have a structure which prevents them from being harmed by the acid in the bodies of the ants.[20]

Woodpeckers, each of whose characteristics is discussed in a different paragraph above, prove with all their detailed features that they are 'created'. If woodpeckers had evolved coincidentally as the theory of evolution claims, they would have died before they acquired such extraordinarily consistent traits and they would be extinct. However, as they were created by Allah with a special 'design' adapted to their life, they started their lives by bearing all the vital characteristics.

### Camouflage

One of the defence strategies of animals is camouflage. Some animals have the special protection of a body structure and coloration which are totally adapted to their habitat. The bodies of these living beings are so harmonious with their environment that when you look at their pictures, you cannot tell if they are plants or animals, or distinguish them from their surroundings.

As will be seen in the following pages, the incredible similarity of an insect to a leaf helps it escape the notice of its enemies. It is obvious that this tiny animal has not made its body look like a leaf. Maybe it is not even aware that it is being protected because it looks like a leaf. However, the camouflage is so deft that it readily impinges as a defence tactic planned specially and 'created'.

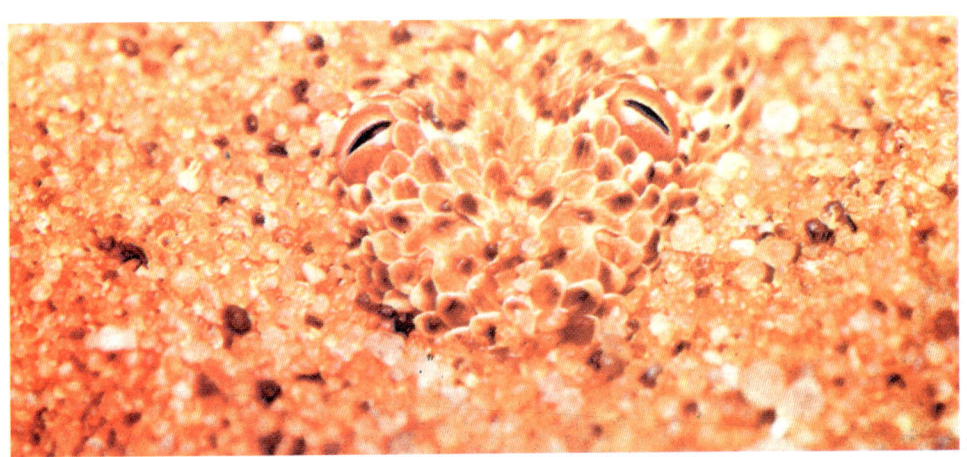

**The snake that camouflages itself in the sand hides from its enemies. Is it possible that this snake made its skin's colour and pattern fully harmonise with its habitat?**

In the picture on the left is a snake hiding among the bushes.

When you look carefully, you will see that what you take to be a tree branch is in fact an insect.

The eggs of a bird called the Western sandpiper are the same colour as their surroundings in order to be protected from enemies.

Some insects disguise themselves as dead leaves. It is quite difficult to distinguish the Panama moth from withered leaves.

This chameleon, known as gecko can assume the colour of its surroundings in 20 minutes.

There is an ant-eater hiding among the leaves! Can you see it?

This caterpillar living in Panamanian rain forests has specks like snake eyes by which it can frighten away predators.

The caterpillar avoids the attention of its enemies because it places its body right in the middle of the leaf.

Armoured chameleons do not change colour according to their environment, because their colour is already created in harmony with their habitat.

This insect species is protected from all its enemies with its leaf-like appearance.

The praying mantis on the orchid has succeeded in deceiving the grasshopper thanks to its wings that look like the petals of the flower.

Insects resembling leaves are very common. It is possible to find all the details of leaves on their bodies.

The snake is camouflaging itself by being poised in the air like all other leaves.

 The tree lice on the left can convince their enemies with their present appearance that they are the thorns of the tree.

## FALSE EYES BEWILDER!

When some butterflies open their wings, we encounter a pair of eyes. These eyes convince their enemies that they are not butterflies. Particularly, the false faces of some butterfly species such as the Shonling butterfly seen above are so perfect with their shiny eyes, facial features, frowning eyebrows, mouth and nose that the overall picture is quite discouraging for many of its enemies. A tenacious person on denying Allah may try to bolster his extraordinary view with the evolutionist explanation of 'an interesting coincidence'. Or he can claim that 'the butterfly brought about this pattern on its body by thinking that it would be useful to it'. If someone makes such a claim and asserts that these patterns that surpass in beauty even the paintings of artists have come about by coincidence, then there is nothing left to say on the part of "the men of understanding". For such a claim is completely incompatible with reason and common sense.

### False Eyes

There are some incredible and unimaginably interesting defence methods in the animal world. One of these is false eyes. With such false eyes, various butterfly, caterpillar and fish species convince their enemies that they are 'dangerous'.

The butterflies in the left pictures open their wings as soon as they sense a danger and display a pair of eyes on each of their wings which appear quite threatening to their enemies.

Let us take our time and think: can these extremely convincing eyes be the result of a coincidence? How does the butterfly know that a pair of scary eyes appear when it opens its wings and that this view would frighten its enemy? Has the butterfly happened to see the pattern on its wings and decided that this pattern was frightening and that it could use it in a moment of danger?

Such a convincing pattern can be the result only of a conscious design, not of coincidences. Moreover, it is by no means possible to think that the butterfly is aware of the patterns on its wings and discovered this as a defence tactic by itself. It is obvious that Allah, Who created the butterfly, bestowed on its body such a pattern and inspired in the animal the instinct to use it in moments of danger.

On the left are the real head and eyes of the thornback ray fish. On the right, the fish swims into its nest and leaves out its tail on which there is a pair of 'eyes'. Other fish around it dare not to come close to it as the false eyes in the tail make them think that it is awake.

*The Signs in the Heavens and on the Earth*

## Water Lilies

Little flowers on the earth are mostly considered commonplace by people, notwithstanding their overall perfection. What prevents people from grasping the creation miracles in these flowers is the familiarity brought about by seeing them everywhere and every day. Therefore, flowers that grow in a totally different place, under totally different conditions and in totally different sizes will be assessed without the 'glasses of familiarity' and thus help us grasp the existence of Allah.

Amazon water lilies that grow in the sticky mud covering the bottom of the Amazon River are interesting enough to remove the 'glasses of familiarity' from people, because they continue their lives not in the way people are accustomed to and witness everyday, but with a very different struggle.

These plants start to grow in the mud at the bottom of the Amazon River, and then reach out towards the river surface. Their goal is to reach the sunlight which is vital to their existence. When they finally reach the water's surface, they stop growing and develop thorny, round buds. The buds develop into gigantic leaves with a reach of 2 metres in as short a time as a couple of hours. 'Knowing' that the more they cover the river sur-

Water lilies can only make use of daylight once they have made their way from the depths of swamps to the water surface by extending upwards as high as 2 metres. However, the roots of these flowers also need oxygen. In the left picture are the stems that stretch out from the roots of the plant to the water surface and carry the oxygen it obtains to the roots.

face with abundant leaves, the more will they be able to make use of sunlight, these water lilies make ample use of daylight to perform photosynthesis. They 'know' that otherwise they will not be able to survive at the bottom of the river due to the scarcity of light. It is certainly quite inspiring for a plant to employ such an 'intelligent' tactic.

However, sunlight alone does not suffice for the Amazon water lilies. They also need oxygen equally, yet it is obvious that this oxygen does not exist in the muddy ground in which their roots are located. This is why water lilies stretch out stems developing from their roots upwards towards the water surface where their leaves float. Sometimes these stems grow as tall as 11 metres; they are tied to the leaves and function as oxygen-carriers between the leaves and the root.[21]

How can a bud in its initial stages in life in the depths of a river know that it needs oxygen and sunlight to survive, that it would not be able to live in their absence, and that everything it needs is present on the water surface? A being recently introduced to life is aware neither of the fact that this water has an ending point, nor of the existence of the sun or oxygen.

Therefore, if the whole event is assessed from the standpoint of evolutionists, these plants should long before have been defeated by environmental conditions and become extinct. Nevertheless, water lilies are still present today in all their perfection.

The unbelievable life struggle of water lilies continues well after they reach light and oxygen on the water surface, where they curl the brims of

*The Signs in the Heavens and on the Earth*

their huge leaves upward to prevent them from sinking.

They can continue their lives with all these precautions, yet they also know that these are not enough for their reproduction. They need a living being that will carry their pollen to another water lily, and this living being is a beetle (coleopterans) which has been created with a special weakness for white colour. They prefer these white water lilies out of all the attractive flowers of the Amazon River. When Amazon water lilies are visited by creatures which will continue their species, they close all their leaves, imprison them, and offer them ample pollen. They let them free after keeping them for one night, and then change their colour so that they do not bring the same pollen back to them. The once pure white, glorious water lilies will now go on adorning the Amazon river in pink.

Could such flawless and finely calculated plans be the work of a bud unaware of everything? Of course not. They are the work of the wisdom of Allah, Who created all things. All the details summarised here show that plants, like all other living beings in the universe, came into existence already furnished with the most convenient systems, and this was thanks to their Creator.

## CONCLUSION

Can the wind form an airplane by coincidence?

The famous physicist Sir Fred Hoyle makes a very striking observation about the origin of life. In his book *The Intelligent Universe* he writes:

> The chance that higher life forms might have emerged in this way (by coincidence) is comparable with the chance that a tornado sweeping through a junk-yard might assemble a Boeing 747 from the materials therein.[22]

This comparison of Hoyle's is quite inspiring. The examples that we have discussed above also reveal that both the existence of life and the perfection of its present systems force us to look for the great power making these come into being. Just as a hurricane cannot produce an airplane as a result of coincidences, neither is it possible for the universe to have come into being as a result of unanticipated happenings and moreover to harbour extremely complex structures therein. In truth, the universe is furnished with myriad systems of an infinitely greater complexity than those of an airplane

Everything we have said in this chapter confronts us with the evidence of the flawless planning not only in our immediate surroundings but also in the depths of space. One who assesses these signs which are so evident as to be undeniable by both reason and conscience can come to only one conclusion: there is no room for coincidence in the universe; the universe was CREATED with all the minutiae contained in it.

And Allah, the Creator of this flawless system, is He Who has infinite might and knowledge.

# Scientists Confirm the Signs of Allah

What we have covered so far shows us that the attributes of the universe discovered by science point to the existence of Allah. Science leads us to the conclusion that the universe has a Creator and this Creator is perfect in might, wisdom and knowledge. It is religion that shows us the way in knowing Allah. It is therefore possible to say that science is a method we use to better see and investigate the realities addressed by religion. Nevertheless, today, some of the scientists who step forth in the name of science take an entirely different stand. In their view, scientific discoveries do not imply the creation of Allah. They have, on the contrary, projected an atheistic understanding of science by saying that it is not possible to reach Allah through scientific data: they claim that science and religion are two clashing notions.

As a matter of fact, this atheistic understanding of science is quite recent. Until a few centuries ago, science and religion were never thought to clash with each other, and science was accepted as a method of proving the existence of Allah. The so-called atheistic understanding of science flourished only after the materialist and positivist philosophies swept through the world of science in the 18th and 19th centuries.

Particularly after Charles Darwin postulated the theory of evolution in 1859, circles holding a materialistic world view started to ideologically defend this theory, which they looked upon as an alternative to religion. The theory of evolution argued that the universe was not created by a creator but came into being by chance. As a result, it was asserted that religion was in conflict with science. The British researchers Michael Baigent, Richard Leigh and Henry Lincoln said on this issue that a century and a half before Darwin, science was not yet divorced from religion and was actually a part of it, its ultimate purpose being to serve it. By Darwin's day, however, science had become detached from religion and defined itself as an absolute rival and alternative to it. These three researchers finally conclude that humanity was from then on forced to make a choice between the two.[23]

As we stated before, the so-called split between science and religion was totally ideological. Some scientists, who earnestly believed in materialism, conditioned themselves to prove that the universe had no creator and they devised various theories in this context. The theory of evolution was the most famous and the most important of them. In the field of astronomy as well certain theories were developed such as the "steady-state theory" or the "chaos theory". However, all of these theories that denied creation were demolished by science itself, as we have clearly shown in the previous chapters.

Today, scientists who still keep to these theories and insist on denying all things religious, are dogmatic and bigoted people, who have conditioned themselves not to believe in Allah. The famous English zoologist and evolutionist D.M.S. Watson confesses to this dogmatism as he explains why he and his colleagues accept the theory of evolution:

> If so, it will present a parallel to the theory of evolution itself, a theory universally accepted, not because it can be proved by logically coherent evidence to be true, but because the only alternative, special creation, is clearly incredible.[24]

What Watson means by "special creation" is Allah's creation. As acknowledged, this scientist finds this "unacceptable". But why? Is it because science says so? Actually it does not. On the contrary, science proves the truth of creation. The only reason why Watson looks upon this fact as unacceptable is because he has conditioned himself to deny the existence of Allah. All other evolutionists take the same stand.

Evolutionists rely not on science but on materialist philosophy and they distort science to make it agree with this philosophy. A geneticist and an outspoken evolutionist from Harvard University, Richard Lewontin, confesses to this truth:

> It is not that the methods and institutions of science somehow compel us to accept a material explanation of the phenomenal world, but, on the contrary, that we are forced by our *a priori* adherence to material causes to create an apparatus of investigation and a set of concepts that produce material explanations, no matter how counter-intuitive, no matter how mystifying to the uninitiated. Moreover, that materialism is absolute, so we cannot allow a Divine Foot in the door.[25]

On the other hand, today, just as in history, there are, as opposed to this dogmatic materialist group, scientists who confirm Allah's existence, and regard science as a way of knowing Him. Some trends developing in the USA such as "Creationism" or "Intelligent Design" prove by scientific evidence that all living things were created by Allah.

This shows us that science and religion are not conflicting sources of information, but that, on the contrary, science is a method that verifies the absolute truths provided by religion. The clash between religion and science can only hold true for certain religions that incorporate some superstitious elements as well as divine sources. However, this is certainly out of the question for Islam, which relies only on the pure revelation of Allah. Moreover, Islam particularly advocates scientific enquiry, and announces that probing the universe is a method to explore the creation of Allah. The following verse of the Qur'an addresses this issue;

> Do they not look at the sky above them? How We have built it and adorned it, and there are no rifts therein? And the earth - We have spread it out, and set thereon mountains standing firm, and caused it to bring forth plants of beauteous kinds (in pairs). And We send down from the sky blessed water whereby We give growth unto gardens and the grain of crops. And tall palm-trees, with shoots of fruit-stalks, piled one over another. (Surah Qaf, 6-7, 9-10)

As the above verses imply, the Qur'an always urges people to think, to reason and to explore everything in the world in which they live. This is because science supports religion, saves the individual from ignorance,

**German physicist Max Planck**  **Sir Isaac Newton**

and causes him to think more consciously; it opens wide one's world of thought and helps one grasp the signs of Allah self-evident in the universe. Prominent German physicist Max Planck said that "everyone who, regardless of his field, studies science seriously is to read the following phrase on the door of the temple of science: 'Have faith'". According to him, faith is an essential attribute of a scientist.[26]

All the issues we have treated so far simply put it that the existence of the universe and all living things cannot be explained by coincidences. Many scientists who have left their mark on the world of science have confirmed, and still confirm this great reality. The more people learn about the universe, the higher does their admiration for its flawless order become. Every newly-discovered detail supports creation in an unquestionable way.

The great majority of modern physicists accept the fact of creation as we set foot in the 21st century. David Darling also maintains that neither time, nor space, nor matter, nor energy, nor even a tiny spot or a cavity existed at the beginning. A slight quick movement and a modest quiver and fluctuation occurred. Darling ends by saying that when the cover of this cosmic box was opened, the tendrils of the miracle of creation appeared from beneath it.[27]

*Scientists Confirm the Signs of Allah*

Besides, it is already known that almost all the founders of diverse scientific branches believed in Allah and His divine books. The greatest physicists in history, Newton, Faraday, Kelvin and Maxwell are a few examples of such scientists.

In the time of Isaac Newton, the great physicist, scientists believed that the movements of the heavenly bodies and planets could be explained by different laws. Nevertheless, Newton believed that the creator of earth and space was the same, and therefore they had to be explained by the same laws. He expanded on this view in his book stating that the perfect system of the sun and planets could only survive under the control and dominance of a mighty and wise being.[28]

As is evident, thousands of scientists who have been doing research in the fields of physics, mathematics, and astronomy since the Middle Ages all agree on the idea that the universe is created by a single Creator and always focus on the same point. The founder of physical astronomy, Johannes Kepler, stated his strong belief in God in one of his books in which he declared that we, as poor, inadequate servants of God, have to see the greatness of God's wisdom and might and submit ourselves to Him.[29]

The great physicist, William Thompson (Lord Kelvin), who founded thermodynamics, was also a Christian who believed in God. He had strongly opposed Darwin's theory of evolution and totally rejected it. He explained shortly before his death that when it looks at the origins of life, science certainly confirms the existence of that Great Power.[30]

One of the professors of physics at Oxford University, Robert Mattheus states the same fact in his book published in 1992 where he explains that DNA molecules were created by God. Mattheus says that all these stages proceed in a perfect harmony from a single cell to a living baby, then to a little child, and finally to an adolescent. All these events can be explained only by a miracle, just as in all the other stages of biology. Mattheus asks how such a perfect and complex organism can emerge from such a simple and tiny cell and how a glorious HUMAN is created from a cell even smaller than the dot on the letter i. He finally concludes that this is nothing short of a miracle.[31]

Some other scientists who admit that the universe is created by a Creator and who are known by their cited attributes are:

Robert Boyle (the father of modern chemistry)

Iona William Petty (known for his studies on statistics and modern economy)

Michael Faraday (one of the greatest physicists of all times)

Gregory Mendel (the father of genetics; he invalidated Darwinism with his discoveries in the science of genetics)

Louis Pasteur (the greatest name in bacteriology; he declared war on Darwinism)

John Dalton (the father of atomic theory)

Blaise Pascal (one of the most important mathematicians)

John Ray (the most important name in British natural history)

Nicolaus Steno (a famous stratigrapher who investigated earth layers)

Carolus Linnaeus (the father of biological classification)

Georges Cuvier (the founder of comparative anatomy)

Matthew Maury (the founder of oceanography)

Thomas Anderson (one the pioneers in the field of organic chemistry)

# Scientific Facts and the Miracle of the Qur'an

The Qur'an was sent down to the earth 14 centuries ago by Allah. The Qur'an is not a book of science. It nonetheless includes some scientific explanations within its religious context. These explanations have never contradicted the findings of modern science. On the contrary, certain facts that could only be discovered with the technology of the 20th century were in fact revealed in the Qur'an 14 centuries ago. This shows us that the Qur'an is one of the most important proofs that proclaims the existence of Allah.

## AN OUTLOOK ON THE UNIVERSE THROUGH THE EYES OF THE QUR'AN

In the light of the data obtained in the 20th century, it has been discovered that the universe came into being suddenly where it was previously non-existent. This theory is known as the Big Bang theory and it holds that the outset of the universe came about with this explosion.

We studied this theory in its historical context backed up by scientific evidence in previous pages under the title "From Non-being to Being". In this chapter, we will see how Allah has declared to us some scientific facts about the creation of the universe in the Qur'an.

There is very strong evidence supporting the Big Bang theory. The expansion of the universe is one of them and the most significant proof of this is the moving away of the galaxies and the heavenly bodies from each other. To better understand, the universe can be thought of as the surface of a balloon being inflated. Just as the points on the surface of a balloon move apart from each other as the balloon is inflated, so do the objects in space move apart from each other as the universe keeps expanding.

At this point, let us refer to the relevant Qur'anic verses. In one verse, the following is stated about the creation of the universe:

> And it is We who have constructed the heaven with might, and verily, it is We who are steadily expanding it. (Surat adh-Dhariyat, 47)

In another verse that refers to the heavens, it is said;

> Do not the Unbelievers see that the heavens and the earth were joined together (as one unit of creation), before We clove them asunder, and We made from water every living thing. Will they not then believe? (Surat al-Anbiya, 30)

The original word "ratk", which is translated as "joined together" in the verse, means "anything close, solid, impervious, united together in a solid mass" according to Arabic dictionaries. That is, it is used for two different pieces that form an entity. The statement "clove asunder" is the "fatk" verb in Arabic and it means to split an object in the state of "ratk". For instance, the sprouting of the seed and the appearance of its shoots on the earth is expressed by this verb.

Now, let us once again look at the verse which refers to a state in which the heavens and the earth are in a state of "ratk". Then, these two are meant to have been cloven asunder in the sense of the verb of "fatk". That is, one of them breaks through the other and makes its way out. Indeed, when we are reminded of the first moment of the Big Bang, we see that the spot called the cosmic egg contained all the matters in the universe. Everything, even "the heavens and the earth" that were not yet created were contained in this spot in a state of "ratk". Afterwards, this cosmic egg exploded, after which all substances became "fatk".

When we compare the expressions in the verse with scientific findings, we see that they are in perfect agreement with each other. Interestingly enough, these findings were not arrived at until the 20th century.

## CREATION OF THE HEAVENS

Steven Weinberg, the author of the book, *The First Three Minutes*, once remarked that a quick glance at the sky might give one the feeling of a strongly "unchanging universe". Indeed, clouds drift along before the moon, the blue vault of heaven turns around the pole star, the moon itself waxes and wanes over a longer period of time, and the moon and the planets move through a plane defined by the stars. We know, however, that all these are local occurrences caused by the movements within our solar system. Weinberg also adds that beyond the planets, the stars seem to be motionless.

Indeed, a quick glance at the sky may give one the feeling that everything is very stable and steady. Yet that is not the case. There is great activity in the sky and this fact, which goes unrecognised by the naked eye, was reported centuries ago in the Qur'an.

There are many verses in the Qur'an that refer to the sky, most of them being plural. The word "semavat", meaning "heavens", in Arabic denotes both the earth's atmosphere and space.

The first point we will discuss here is the plural use of the word "heavens". This plural use is one of the miracles of the Qur'an. Let us now explain why.

Assume that you go out into the open air and turn your head up towards the sky. What will you see? If it is summer, you will see either a bright blue sky or some clouds floating in the wind; and if winter, a grey, hazy sky covered with clouds. Whatever you see, you will not be able to see the atmosphere surrounding the world. You can never know that this atmosphere is made up of several layers. That the Qur'an makes reference to this detail unobservable by the naked eye is a great piece of evidence that it is the word of Allah:

> He Who has created seven heavens in full harmony with one another: no incongruity will you see in the creation of the Most Gracious. And turn your vision (upon it) once more: can you see any flaw? Yes, turn your vision (upon it) again and yet again: (and every time) your vision will fall back upon you, dazzled and truly defeated. (Surat al-Mulk, 3-4)

The Originator is He of the heavens and the earth: and when He wills a thing to be, He but says unto it, "Be" – and it is.
(Surat al-Baqara, 117)

Space may be imagined as an enormous cavity: an infinitely vast cavity, a cavity containing stars, planets and bodies in motion. However, space is not a cavity left to itself. It is a "system" consisting of countless stars, solar systems, planets, satellites and comets. It was earlier stated in the Qur'an that the sky and space were created flawlessly within "a great order":

> Do they not look at the sky above them? How We have built it and adorned it, and there are no rifts therein? (Surah Qaf, 6)

## STARS AND PLANETS

Let us first look at what is meant by the word "star" in the Qur'an. The stars denoted by the words "necm" (star) and "kandil" (lamp) in the Qur'an have two main functions as implied in the verses. They are a source of light and they are used for navigation.

Particularly in the verses depicting the resurrection day, it is stressed that the lights of the stars are put out and become dim. When the sun, which is a star as well is referred to, the word "kandil "is used. The word "kandil" is also used when referring to the stars adorning the sky. Yet a very important distinction is made where the word "nur" (light) is used for the moon. In this way, the stars and the objects that are not stars are distinguished from one another. This fact, which could not have been known 14 centuries ago, is one of the miracles of the Qur'an.

We had mentioned that the second function of the stars as they are referred to in the verses is as a guide to navigation. These verses make it plain that people can determine the right direction by the help of the stars in the sky. In all of these verses, the word "necm" is used. Indeed, before the invention of the compass, which has a very significant role at the outset of the geographical discoveries in the Middle Ages, navigation was only possible with the help of the stars on night voyages.

How is it possible that the stars show direction? It is possible only if they are arranged in an observable order in their fixed places. If a star appeared in one place one night, and in another the next, it would be impossible to find one's way by it. In this context, the particular places where the stars appear in the sky have great importance. In the Qur'an,

Allah says:

> Nay, I swear by the places of the stars And behold! that verily is a tremendous oath, if you but knew. (Surat al-Waqia, 75-76)

## THE SUN AND THE MOON

There are many verses in the Qur'an that make mention of the sun and the moon. An interesting property is revealed when their Arabic wording is investigated. In the verses, the words "sirac" (lamp) and "vahhac" (brightly-burning) are used for the sun. For the moon, the word "munir" (enlightening, shiny) is used. Indeed, while the sun produces an enormous amount of heat and light as a result of the nuclear reactions inside, the moon merely reflects the light it receives from the sun. The verses make reference to this distinction as follows:

> Do you not see how God has created seven heavens in full harmony with one another, and has made the moon a light therein, and made the sun a (radiant) lamp? (Surah Nuh, 15-16)

> We have built above you seven strong heavens, and have placed (therein the sun), a lamp full of blazing splendour. (Surat an-Naba, 12-13)

> Blessed Is He Who has set up in the skies constellations, and has placed among them a (radiant) lamp and a light-giving moon. (Surat al-Furqan, 61)

The difference between the sun and the moon is quite evident in the verses. One is depicted as a source of light and the other as a light-reflecting agent. It is impossible for such a detail to have been known at that time. It was not until centuries later that men came into possession of this knowledge. Therefore, the fact that this information was already given in the Qur'an is one of the proofs that the Qur'an was revealed by God.

Now, let us turn our attention to another magnificent characteristic of the heavenly bodies - which is their movements in space.

By the sky full of paths and orbits.
(Surat adh-Dhariyat, 7)

## ORBITS DESCRIBED IN THE QUR'AN

Above, we have stated that the heavenly bodies are in motion in space. These movements are fully controlled and all bodies move in a computed orbit. In the Qur'an, certain verses referring to the sun and the moon run as follows: "The sun and the moon follow courses (exactly) computed". (Surat ar-Rahman, 5) "It is not for the sun to catch up the moon, nor does the night outstrip the day. Each (just) swims along in (its own) orbit." (Surah Yasin, 40) Another verse to the same effect declares:

> It is He Who created the night and the day, and the sun and the moon. They swim along, each in an orbit. (Surat al-Anbiya, 33)

According to a currently acknowledged theory, massive and voluminous bodies in the universe exert a gravitational force on smaller bodies. For example, the moon makes an orbit around the earth, which has a bigger volume. The earth and other planets in the solar system move in an orbit around the sun. There exists a still bigger system around which the solar system makes an orbit. The most critical point in all these details is that none of the stars, planets and other bodies in space make an uncontrolled move, cut across each other's orbit, or hit one another.

The Qur'an signifies the harmonious movement of these bodies as follows:

> By the sky full of paths and orbits. (Surat adh-Dhariyat, 7)

The sun, as one of the billions of stars in the universe, travels more than 17 million kilometers a day in space. This journey of the sun is referred to by Allah as follows:

> And the sun runs on unto a resting-place for him. That is the decree of (Him), the Exalted in Might, the All-Knowing. (Surah Yasin, 38)

## THE CANOPY WELL GUARDED

> We have made the sky a canopy well guarded and (yet) they turn aside from its signs. (Surat al-Anbiya, 32)

Almost everyone has seen the pictures of the moon's surface. The surface structure is very uneven due to the countless meteors that have fallen on it. The multitude of craters formed by these meteors is one of the most peculiar characteristics of the moon. Any space station or residential site established on the moon surface with no special shield would very likely be razed to the ground before long. The only way to prevent this is to "guard" it in some way.

This detail, which we almost never think about, is provided for the earth in a very natural way. There is therefore no need for people to take extra measures to survive. The atmosphere of the earth destroys all meteors big and small approaching the earth, filters the harmful rays in space and thus carries out a vital process for the permanence of human life.

Many detrimental - and even fatal - rays reach the earth from the sun and other stars. In particular, the energy explosions, the so-called "flares" that take place in the sun, the closest star to the earth, constitute the main source of these harmful rays.

During these sun flashes, a plasma cloud is thrown into space with an average speed of 1,500 km/second. The plasma cloud, made up of positively charged protons and negatively charged electrons, is electrically conductive. As the cloud approaches the earth with a speed of 1,500 kms/second, it begins to produce an electric current under the effect of the magnetic field around the earth. On the other hand, the magnetic field of the earth exerts a pushing force on the plasma cloud that has a current flowing through it. This force stops the movement of the cloud and keeps it at a certain distance. Let us now take a look at the power of the plasma cloud that is "stopped" before reaching the earth.

Although the plasma cloud is arrested by the magnetic field of the earth, its effects are still perceived from the earth. Following strong flashes, transformers may explode in high voltage lines, communication networks may be damaged or electric network fuses may blow out.

In a sun-spot explosion, the energy released is calculated to be equivalent to 100 billion times that of the atom bomb dropped on Hiroshima. Fifty-eight hours after the flash, extreme activity was observed on the needle of the compass, and the heat jumped up to $2,500^0$ C at a level about 250 kilometers above the atmosphere.

Yet another particle current is diffused from the sun with a relatively lower speed, approximately 400 km/second. This is called the "solar wind". Solar winds are controlled by a layer of charged particles called the "Van Allen Radiation Belt" which is produced under the effect of the magnetic field of the earth, and thus they cause no harm to the world. The formation of this layer is made possible by the characteristics of the world's core. The core contains magnetic metals like iron and nickel. What is more important is that the nucleus is made up of two different structures. The inner core is solid while the outer core is fluid. These two layers of the core move around each other. This movement creates a magnetic effect in metals which leads to the formation of a magnetic field. The Van Allen Belt is an extension of this magnetic field that stretches to the outermost reaches of the atmosphere. This magnetic field protects the earth against the dangers likely to come from space. Solar winds cannot pass through the Van Allen Belt, 40,000 miles from the earth. When in the form of electrically charged particles they meet this magnetic field, they decompose and flow around the belt.

**If "the canopy well guarded" had not existed, the dangers awaiting the earth would unquestionably not be as few as those in the picture.**

*Scientific Facts and the Miracle of the Qur'an*

Just like the Van Allen Belt, the earth's atmosphere also protects the earth from the destructive effects of space. We mentioned that the atmosphere protects the earth from meteors. However, this is not the only characteristic of the atmosphere. For instance, a -273 temperature temperature in outer space, which is called "absolute zero" would have a fatal effect on people, were it not for the permanently higher temperatures of the earth is atmosphere.

What is more interesting is that the atmosphere lets only harmless rays, radio waves and visible light in, because these are vital elements for life. The ultraviolet rays, which are only partially let in by the atmosphere are very important for the photosynthesis of plants and for the survival of all living beings. This radiation, which is very strongly emitted from the sun to the earth, is filtered through the ozone layer of the atmosphere and only a limited required portion of it reaches the earth. The sun's rays are one of the most essential requirements of life.

Briefly, there is an excellent system at work on the earth which encompasses itself and protects it from outer dangers. In the Qur'an, the shielded state of the earth is revealed by the following verse:

> And We have made the heavens a canopy well guarded: (yet) they turn aside from its signs. (Surat al-Anbiya, 32)

There is no doubt that in the 7th century, it was impossible to have known either about the protective quality of the atmosphere, or the existence of the Van Allen Belt. However, the expression "a canopy well guarded" perfectly explains the protective agents around the earth that have not been discovered until modern times. So the above verse referring to the heavens as "a canopy well guarded" indicates that the Qur'an was sent by a Creator Who has knowledge of everything and acknowledges all.

## THE RELATIVITY OF TIME

The relativity of time is a proven scientific fact today. However, until Einstein put it as the "theory of relativity" early this century, no one ever thought that time could be relative and contingent on velocity and mass.

With a single exception though! The Qur'an yielded information about the relativity of time! Three related verses are;

> Yet they ask you to hasten on the Punishment! But Allah will not fail in His Promise. Verily a Day in the sight of your Lord is like a thousand years of your reckoning. (Surat al-Hajj, 47)

> He regulates the affair from the heaven to the earth; then shall it ascend to Him in a day the measure of which is a thousand years of what you count. (Surat al-Sajda, 5)

> The angels and the spirit ascend unto him in a Day the measure whereof is (as) fifty thousand years. (Surat al-Maarij, 4)

As a book whose revelation began in 610, the Qur'an's referring to relativity so straightforwardly is another evidence that it is a divine book.

## THE ROUNDNESS OF THE EARTH

Arabic, the language in which the Qur'an was revealed, is a very rich and developed language. Its vocabulary is very large and words have many variations. For this reason, some of the verbs in Arabic cannot be translated into some languages as single words. For instance, the verb "hashiya" means "fearing with awe" (other words are used for other types of fears). Or the word "karia" is used for referring to "an adversity, that which strikes", that is, the day of Resurrection.

One of these verbs is "tekvir". In English, this means "to make one thing lap over another, folded up as a garment that is laid away". For instance, in Arabic dictionaries this word is used for the action of wrapping one thing around another, in the way that a turban is put on. Let us now look at a verse where the verb "tekvir" is used:

> He has created the Heavens and the Earth for Truth. He wraps the night up in the day, and wraps the day up in the night. (Surat az-Zumar, 5)

The information given in the verse about the day's and the night's wrapping each other up includes accurate information about the shape of the world. This situation can be true only if the earth is round. This means that in the Qur'an, the roundness of the world was hinted at.

However, the understanding of astronomy of the time perceived the world differently. As we have mentioned, it was then thought that the

He it is Who has made the earth subservient unto you, so walk in the paths thereof and eat of His providence. And to Him is the return after death. (Surat al-Mulk, 15)

world was a flat plane and all scientific calculations and explanations were based on this belief. However, since the Qur'an is Allah's word, the most correct words are used in it while describing the universe.

## THE FUNCTION OF MOUNTAINS

According to geological findings, the mountains have arisen as a result of the movements and clashes of huge plates constituting the crust of the earth. These plates are enormously big and carry all the continents. When two plates collide, one usually slides under the other and the debris in between is raised up. The big curves in the compressed debris form the mountains by being elevated higher than their surroundings. In the meantime, the protrusion that constitutes mountains proceeds under the ground as well as over the ground. That means that mountains have a portion stretching downwards as large as their visible portion. These extensions of mountains below ground prevent the crust of the earth from sliding on the magma layer or between its own layers.

As this explanation makes clear, one of the most significant characteristics of mountains is their formation at the conjunction points of the earth's plates that are closely pressed together as they come near and their "fixing" them. That is, we may liken mountains to nails that keep wood pieces together.

Moreover, the pressure the mountains exert on the crust of the earth with their enormous mass prevents the magma movements in the core of the earth from reaching the earth and destroying the earth's crust. The central layer of the earth, called the core, is an area made up of substances melted in temperatures rising to thousands of degrees. Movements in the core cause detachment regions to form between the plates making up the earth. The mountains that form in these regions obstruct the upward movements and protect the world from violent earthquakes.

It is very interesting to note that these technical facts discovered by modern geology in our day were revealed in the Qur'an centuries ago. In a verse on the mountains, it is declared in the Qur'an:

He created the heavens without any pillars that you can see; He set on

> the earth mountains standing firm, lest it should shake with you; and He scattered through it beasts of all kinds. (Surat al-Luqman, 30)

With this verse, the Qur'an denied a superstitious belief that was commonly accepted at the time. Having a primitive astronomical knowledge like many other communities of the time, Arabs thought that the heavens were raised high above the mountains. (This was a traditional belief which was subsequently added to the explanation of the universe in the Old Testament.) This belief held that there were high mountains at the two ends of a flat world. These were the "buttresses" of the heavens. They were thought to be pillars that held the heavens above in their place. The verse above disproved this and maintained that the heavens were "without any buttresses". The real geological function of the mountains was also disclosed: to prevent tremors. Another verse stresses the same point:

> And We have set on the earth mountains standing firm, lest it should shake with them, and We have made therein broad highways (between mountains) for them to pass through: that they may receive Guidance. (Surat al-Anbiya, 31)

## RAIN

Rain is indeed one of the most important factors for the permanence of life on earth. It is a prerequisite for the continuation of activity in a region. Rain, which carries great importance for all living things, including human beings, is mentioned in various verses of the Qur'an, where substantial information is given about the formation of rain, its proportion and effects. This information, which never could have been known by the people of the time, shows us that the Qur'an is the word of Allah.

Now, let us examine the information given in the Qur'an about rain.

### The Proportion of Rain

In the eleventh verse of Surat az-Zukhruf, rain is defined as water sent down in "due measure". The verse is as follows:

> He sends down (from time to time) water from the sky in due measure, and We raise to life therewith a land that is dead. Even so will you be

raised (from the dead). (Surat az-Zukhruf, 11)

This "measure" mentioned in the verse has to do with a couple of characteristics of rain. First of all, the amount of rain that falls on the earth is always the same. It is estimated, that in one second, 16 million tonnes of water evaporate from the earth. This number is equal to the amount of water that drops on the earth in one second. This means that water continuously circulates in a balanced cycle according to a "measure".

Another measure related with rain is about its falling speed. The minimum altitude of rain clouds is 1,200 meters. When dropped from this height, an object having the same weight and size as a rain drop, would continuously accelerate and fall on the ground with a speed of 558 km/h. Certainly, any object that hits the ground with that speed would cause great damage. If rain happened to fall in the same way, all harvested lands would be destroyed, residential areas, houses, and cars would be damaged, and people would not be able to walk around without taking extra precautions. What is more, these calculations are made just for clouds at a height of 1,200 meters; there are also rain clouds at altitudes of 10,000 meters. A rain drop falling from such a height could normally reach a very destructive speed.

But this is not how it works; no matter from what height they fall, the average speed of rain drops is only 8-10 km/h when they reach the ground. The reason for this is the special form they take. This special form increases the friction effect of the atmosphere and prevents acceleration when the rain drops reach a certain speed "limit". (Today parachutes are designed by using this technique.)

This is not all about the "measures" of rain. For instance, in the atmospheric layers where it starts to rain, the temperature may fall as low as $40^0$ C below zero. Despite this, rain drops never turn into ice particles. (This would certainly mean a fatal threat to the living things on the earth.) The reason is that the water in the atmosphere is pure water. As is well-known, pure water hardly freezes even at very low temperatures.

### The Formation of Rain

How rain forms remained a great mystery for people for a long time. Only after weather radar was invented, was it possible to discover the stages by which rain is formed.

The formation of rain takes place in three stages. First, the "raw material" of rain rises up into the air. Later clouds are formed. Finally, rain drops appear.

These stages are clearly defined in the Qur'an centuries ago where precise information is given about the formation of rain:

> It is Allah Who sends the Winds, and they raise the Clouds: then does He spread them in the sky as He wills, and break them into fragments, until you see rain-drops issue from the midst thereof: then when He has made them reach such of his servants as He wills, behold, they do rejoice! (Surat ar-Room, 48)

Now, let us look at the three stages mentioned in the verse;

**1ST STAGE:** "It is Allah Who sends the winds..."

Countless air bubbles formed by the foaming in the oceans continuously burst and cause water particles to be ejected towards the sky. These particles, which are rich in salt, are then carried away by winds and move upwards in the atmosphere. These particles, which are called aerosols, form clouds by collecting around themselves the water vapour, which again ascends from the seas, as tiny drops by a mechanism called "water trap"

**2ND STAGE:** " ...and they raise the Clouds: then does He spread them in the sky as He wills, and break them into fragments..."

The clouds form from the water vapour that condenses around the salt crystals or the dust particles in the air. Because the water drops in these are very small (with a diameter between 0.01 and 0.02 mm), the clouds are suspended in the air and they spread in the sky. Thus the sky is covered with clouds.

**3RD STAGE:** "...until you see rain-drops issue from the midst thereof."

Water particles that surround salt crystals and dust particles thicken and form rain drops. So, the drops, which become heavier than air, depart from the clouds, and start to fall on the ground as rain.

Every stage in the formation of rain is told in the verses of the Qur'an. Furthermore, these stages are explained in the right sequence. Just as with many other natural phenomena in the world, it is again the Qur'an that provides the most correct explanation about this phenomena as well, and more, that has announced these facts to people centuries before they were discovered by science.

### Life Given to a Dead Land

In the Qur'an, many verses call our attention to a particular function of rain, which is "giving life to a dead land":

> We send down pure water from the sky. That with it We may give life to a dead land, and slake the thirst of many beings We have created, beasts as well as humans. (Surat al-Furqan, 48- 49)

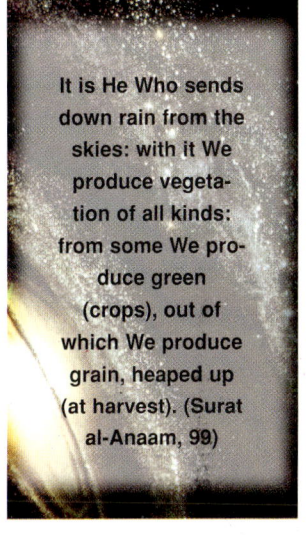

It is He Who sends down rain from the skies: with it We produce vegetation of all kinds: from some We produce green (crops), out of which We produce grain, heaped up (at harvest). (Surat al-Anaam, 99)

In addition to furnishing the earth with water, which is an inevitable need of living beings, rain also has a fertilisation effect.

Rain drops that reach the clouds after being evaporated from the seas, contain certain substances "that will give life" to a dead land. These "life-giving" drops are called "surface tension drops". Surface tension drops form on the top level of the sea surface which is called the "micro layer" by biologists. In this layer, which is thinner than one tenth of a millimetre, there are many organic leftovers caused by the pollution of microscopic algae and zooplankton. Some of these leftovers select and collect within themselves some elements which are very rare in sea water, such as phosphorus, magnesium, potassium and some heavy metals like copper, zinc, cobalt and lead. These "fertiliser"-laden drops are lifted up into the sky by the winds and after a while they drop on the ground inside the rain drops. Seeds and plants on the earth find numerous metallic salts and elements essential for their growth here in these rain drops. This event is revealed

*Scientific Facts and the Miracle of the Qur'an*

It is He who sends down water from the sky: from it you drink, and out of it (grows) the vegetation on which you feed your cattle. With it He produces for you corn, olives, date-palms, grapes and every kind of fruit: verily in this is a sign for those who give thought. (Surat an-Nahl, 10-11)

in another verse of the Qur'an:

> And We send down from the sky rain laden with blessing, and We produce therewith gardens and grain for harvests. (Surah Qaf, 9)

Salts that fall with rain are small examples of certain elements (calcium, magnesium, potassium, etc.) used for increasing fertility. The heavy metals found in these types of aerosols are other elements that increase fertility in the development and production of plants.

A barren land can be furnished with all the essential elements for plants in a 100-year period just with these fertilisers dropped with the rain. Forests also develop and are fed with the help of these sea-based aerosols. In this way, 150 million tons of fertiliser falls on the total land surface every year. If there were no natural fertilisation like this, there would be very little vegetation on the earth, and the ecological balance would be impaired.

What is more interesting is that this truth, which could only be discovered by modern science, was revealed by Allah in the Qur'an centuries ago.

## FECUNDATING WINDS

In the Qur'an, the winds are revealed as "fecundating":

> And We send the fecundating winds, then cause water to descend from the sky, therewith providing you with water (in abundance). (Surat al-Hijr, 22)

In Arabic, the word "fecundating" implies the fecundating of both plants and clouds. Accordingly, modern science has shown that winds indeed have both of these functions. Winds, as mentioned before, do fecundate clouds by carrying the crystals that are to take part in the formation of rain drops. On the other hand, they also fecundate plants.

Plants throw pollen seeds containing sperm cells into the air. Most plants are ideally created to catch the pollen from the wind. Cones, hanging flowers, and some other plants make canals that open towards air currents, which carry these seeds to other plants of the same species. Pollen seeds containing sperm cells arrive at the reproductive organs thanks to these canals. The pollen reaching the ovule fertilises the egg and thus ovules turn into seeds.

Most plants are ideally created to catch pollen from the wind. Cones, hanging flowers, and some others make canals that open towards air currents. Sperm-producing pollens arrive at reproductive regions thanks to these canals. Plants throw sperm-producing pollen seeds into the air. Afterwards, air currents carry these seeds to other plants of the same species. The pollen reaching the ovule fertilises the egg and thus ovules turn into seeds.

## THE UNIQUENESS OF THE FINGERPRINT

The "fingerprint" which is formed on the tip of the finger by the visible pattern the skin takes is absolutely unique to its owner. Every person living on the earth has a different set of fingerprints. All the people who have lived throughout history also had different fingerprints. These prints remain unchanged throughout one's lifetime unless a great injury occurs.

That is why the fingerprint is accepted as a very important identity card and used for this purpose around the world.

However, two centuries ago, the fingerprint was not so important, because it was only discovered in the late 19th century that all fingerprints are different from one another. In 1880, an English scientist named Henry Faulds stated in an article published in *Nature* that the fingerprints of people did not change throughout their lives, and that suspects could be convicted by the fingerprints they left on surfaces such as glass.[32] In 1884, for the first time a murder was solved by means of identifying fingerprints. Since then, fingerprints have become an important method of identification. Before the 19th century, however, people most probably had never thought that the wavy shapes on their fingertips had any meaning or considered them worthy of note.

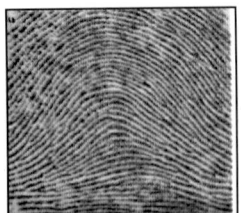 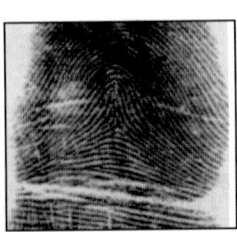 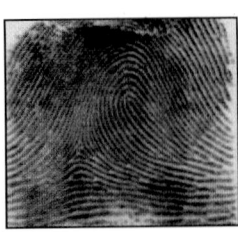 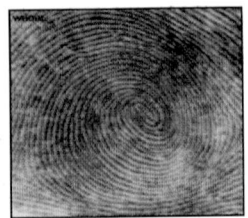

**The fingerprints of every person who has ever lived are different.**

In the 7th century, the Qur'an pointed out that the fingertips of human beings bore an important characteristic:

> Does man think that We cannot assemble his bones? Yes, We are able to put together in perfect order the very tips of his fingers. (Surat al-Qiyama, 3-4)

## THE BIRTH OF MAN

Many diverse subjects are mentioned in the Qur'an in the course of inviting people to believe. Sometimes the heavens, sometimes the animals, and sometimes the plants are shown as evidence to man by Allah. In many of the verses, people are called upon to turn their attention to their own creation. They are often reminded how man has come into the world, which stages he has passed through and what his essence is:

> It is We Who have created you. Why, then, do you not accept the truth? Have you ever considered that (seed) which you emit? Is it you who create it? Or are We the Creator? (Surat al-Waqia, 57-59)

The creation of man and the miraculous aspect of this is stressed in many other verses. Some bits of information within these verses are so detailed that it is impossible for a person living in the 7th century to have known them. Some of them are as follows:

1. Man is not created from the complete semen, but from a very small portion of it (sperm).
2. It is the male that determines the sex of the baby.
3. The human embryo adheres to the uterus of the mother like a leech.
4. The human develops in three dark regions in the uterus.

People living in the age when the Qur'an was revealed, to be sure, knew that the basic substance of birth was related to the semen of the male emitted during sexual intercourse. And the fact that the baby was born after a nine-month period was obviously an observable event not calling for any further investigation. However, the bits of information quoted above were far above the level of learning of the people living in that period. These could only be verified by 20th century science.

Now, let us go over them one by one.

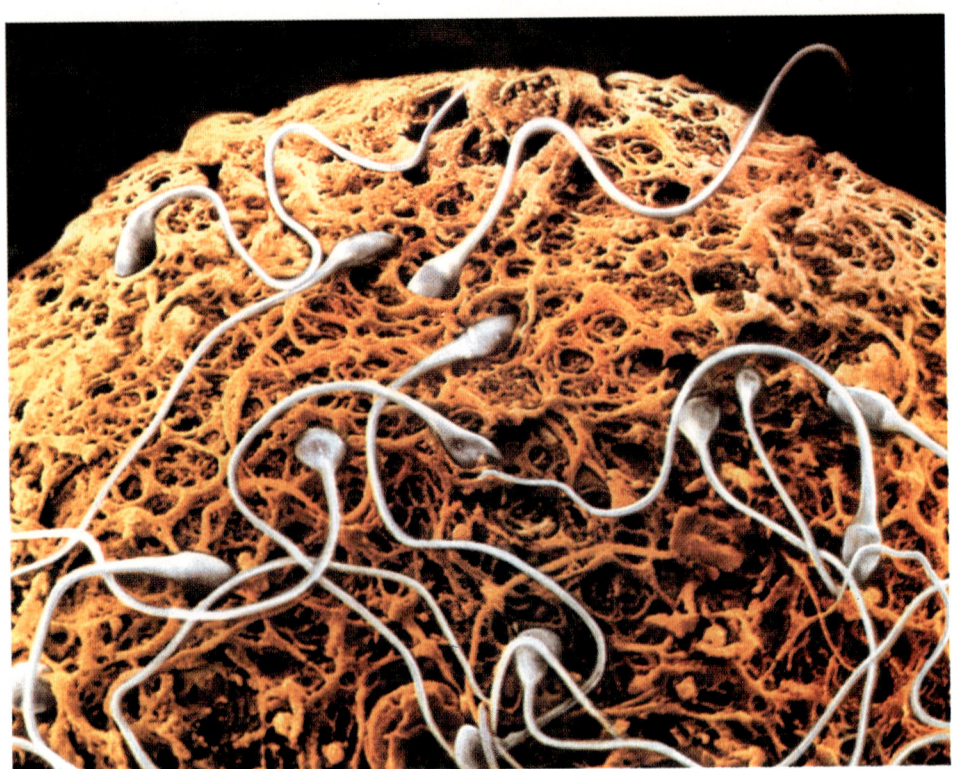

Sperms surrounding the ovum

### A Drop of Semen

During sexual intercourse, 250 million sperms are emitted from the male at a time. The sperms undertake an arduous 5-minute journey in the mother's body until they make it to the ovum. Only a thousand out of 250 million sperms succeed in reaching the ovum. The ovum, the size of half a grain of salt, will let only one of the sperms in. That is, the essence of man is not the whole semen but only a small portion of it. This is explained in the Qur'an:

> Does man think that he will be left uncontrolled, (without purpose)? Was he not a drop of sperm emitted (in lowly form)? (Surat al-Qiyama, 36-37)

As we have seen, the Qur'an informs us that man is made not from the complete semen but only a small part of it. That the particular emphasis in this statement announces a fact only discovered by modern science is evidence that the statement is divine in origin.

### The Mixture in the Semen

The fluid called semen does not consist of sperms alone. On the contrary, it is made up of a mixture of different fluids. These fluids have functions such as containing the sugar necessary for providing energy for the sperms, neutralising the acids at the entrance of the uterus and creating the slippery environment for the easy movement of the sperms.

Interestingly enough, when semen is mentioned in the Qur'an, this fact, which is discovered by modern science, is also referred to and the semen is defined as a mixed fluid:

Verily We created Man from a drop of mingled sperm, in order to try him: So We gave him (the gifts), of hearing and sight. (Surat al-Insan, 2)

In another verse, the semen is again referred to as a mixture and it is stressed that man is created from the "essence" of this mixture:

He Who has made everything which He has created most good: He began the creation of man with clay, and made his progeny from a quintessence of the nature of a fluid despised. (Surat al-Sajda, 7-8)

The Arabic word "sulala", translated as "quintessence", means the essential or best part of something. By either implication, it means "part of a whole". This shows that the Qur'an is the word of a Will that knows the creation of man down to its slightest detail. This Will is the Creator of man.

### Determining a Baby's Sex

Until fairly recently it was thought that a baby's sex was determined by the male and female genes together. The improving disciplines of genetics and microbiology proved in the 20th century that the female has no role in the process.

Two of the 46 chromosomes that determine the structure of a human being are the sex chromosomes. These chromosomes are called "XY" in males and "XX" in females, because the shapes of the chromosomes resemble these letters. The Y chromosome is the one that carries all the specifically male genes.

The formation of an infant starts by the uniting of two chromosomes: one from the father and one from the mother. Because a female only has

> Were they created of nothing, or were they themselves the creators? Or did they create the heavens and the earth? Nay, they have no firm belief.
> (Surat at-Tur, 35-36)

X chromosomes, her reproductive cells (ova) will contain only those. Males on the other hand, have both X and Y chromosomes, so half of their reproductive cells (sperms) will be X and the other half Y. If an ovum unites with a sperm containing an X chromosome, the offspring is female; if it unites with one containing a Y chromosome, the offspring is male.

In other words, a baby's sex is determined by which (X or Y) chromosome from the male unites with the chromosome from the female.

None of this was known until the discovery of genetics in the 20th century. Indeed, in many cultures it was believed that a baby's sex was determined by the condition (health, etc.) of the mother's body. That was why women were blamed when they had girls. (This primitive belief is still common.)

Thirteen centuries before the genes were discovered, the Qur'an, however, revealed information that denies this. In a verse it is stated that maleness or femaleness is created from a drop of semen: that is, the source of the sexes is not the woman but the man.

> ... He did create in pairs, male and female, from a drop of sperm as it is poured forth. (Surat an-Najm, 45-46)

### The Clot Clinging to the Uterus

When the sperm of the male unites with the ovum of the female as described above, the essence of the baby to be born is formed. This single cell, known as the "zygote" in biology, will instantly start to reproduce by dividing and eventually become a "piece of flesh".

The zygote, however, does not spend its developmental period in a void. It clings to the uterus just like roots that are firmly fixed to the earth by their tendrils. Through this bond, the zygote can obtain the substances essential to its development from the mother's body.

Such a detail could not have been known without a sound knowledge of medicine. It is obvious that no one possessed such knowledge 14 centuries ago. Interestingly enough, Allah always refers to the zygote developing in the mother's womb as "a clot of blood" in the Qur'an:

> Read! In the name of your Sustainer, who has created man from a clot. Read – for your Sustainer is the Most Bounteous. (Surat al-Alaq, 1-3)

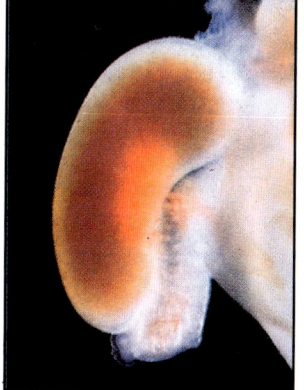

**A zygote that has clung on to the uterus in the form of a piece of flesh.**

*Scientific Facts and the Miracle of the Qur'an*

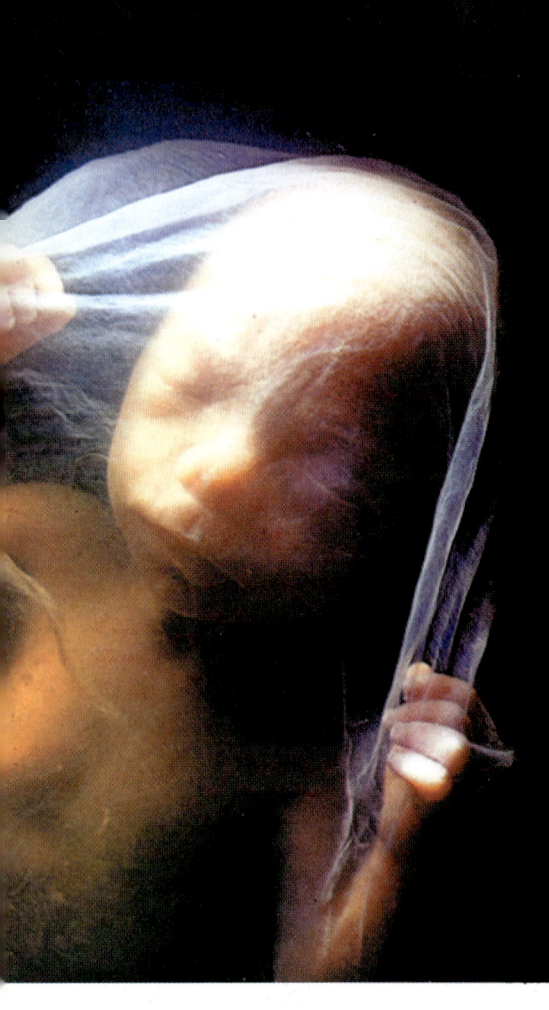

**O man! What has beguiled you from your bountiful Sustainer? Him Who created you, fashioned you in due proportion, and gave you a just bias. In whatever form He willed, He put you together. (Surat al-Infitar, 6-8)**

Does man think that he will be left uncontrolled, (without purpose)? Was he not a drop of sperm emitted (in lowly form)? Then he became a clot; then Allah made and fashioned him in due proportion. And made of him a pair, the male and the female. (Surat al-Qiyama, 36-39)

The Arabic meaning of the word "clot" is "a thing that clings to some place". The word is literally used to describe leeches that cling to a body to suck blood. It is obviously the best word possible to describe the zygote that clings to the wall of the uterus and absorbs its sustenance from it.

The Qur'an has more to disclose about the zygote.

Perfectly clinging to the uterus, the zygote starts to develop. The uterus of the mother, meanwhile, is filled with a fluid called the "amnion liquid" that surrounds the zygote. The most important feature of the amnion liquid in which the baby develops is to protect the baby against blows coming from outside. In the Qur'an, this fact is revealed as follows:

> Did We not create you from a base fluid which We placed in a safe place, firmly fixed? (Surat al-Mursalat, 20-21)

All this information given in the Qur'an about the formation of man demonstrates that the Qur'an came from a source that knows about this formation down to its slightest detail.

This once more proves that the Qur'an is the word of Allah. It would be sheer nonsense to claim that the information yielded by the Qur'an about birth is "coincidentally" correct: for there are many details revealed in the Qur'an and such a detailed account has no chance whatsoever of "coincidentally" agreeing with the truth in every respect.

Every description of the Qur'an is true because every verse of it is comprised of the words of Allah. Since it is Allah Who has created and shaped man in the mother's womb, to Him belong the words that best describe this process. Allah Who has created all of us in like manner describes the outset of our lives in another verse as follows:

> Man We did create from a quintessence of clay. Then We placed him as (a drop of) sperm in a safe place of rest. Then We made the drop a clot; then of that clot We made a lump of flesh; then we made out of that lump of flesh bones and clothed the bones with flesh; then we brought this into being as a new creation. So blessed be Allah, the best to create! (Surat al-Mumenoon, 12-14)

# PART 2

### THOSE WHO ARE UNABLE TO SEE

# THE FACT OF CREATION

# Evolution Deceit

The theory of evolution is a philosophy and a conception of the world that produces false hypotheses, assumptions and imaginary scenarios in order to explain the existence and origin of life in terms of mere coincidences. The roots of this philosophy go back as far as antiquity and ancient Greece.

All atheist philosophies that deny creation, directly or indirectly embrace and defend the idea of evolution. The same condition today applies to all the ideologies and systems that are antagonistic to religion.

The evolutionary notion has been cloaked in a scientific disguise for the last century and a half in order to justify itself. Though put forward as a supposedly scientific theory during the mid-19th century, the theory, despite all the best efforts of its advocates, has not so far been verified by any scientific finding or experiment. Indeed, the "very science" on which the theory depends so greatly has demonstrated and continues to demonstrate repeatedly that the theory has no merit in reality.

Laboratory experiments and probabilistic calculations have definitely made it clear that the amino acids from which life arises cannot have been formed by chance. The cell, which supposedly emerged by chance under primitive and uncontrolled terrestrial conditions according to evolutionists, still cannot be synthesised even in the most sophisticated, high-tech laboratories of the 20th century. Not a single "transitional form", creatures which are supposed to show the gradual evolution of advanced organisms from more primitive ones as neo-Darwinist theory claims, has ever been found anywhere in the world despite the most diligent and prolonged search in the fossil record.

Striving to gather evidence for evolution, evolutionists have unwittingly proven by their own hands that evolution cannot have happened at all!

The person who originally put forward the theory of evolution, essentially in the form that it is defended today, was an amateur English biologist by the name of Charles Robert Darwin. Darwin first published his ideas in a book entitled *The Origin of Species by Means of Natural Selection* in 1859. Darwin claimed in his book that all living beings had a common ancestor and that they evolved from one another by means of natural selection. Those that best adapted to the habitat transferred their traits to subsequent generations, and by accumulating over great epochs, these advantageous qualities transformed individuals into totally different species from their ancestors. The human being was thus the most developed product of the mechanism of natural selection. In short, the origin of one species was another species.

Darwin's fanciful ideas were seized upon and promoted by certain ideological and political circles and the theory became very popular. The main reason was that the level of knowledge of those days was not yet sufficient to reveal that Darwin's imaginary scenarios were false. When Darwin put forward his assumptions, the disciplines of genetics, microbiology, and biochemistry did not yet exist. If they had, Darwin might easily have recognised that his theory was totally unscientific and thus would not have attempted to advance such meaningless claims: the information determining species already exists in the genes and it is impossible for natural selection to produce new species by altering genes.

While the echoes of Darwin's book reverberated, an Austrian botanist by the name of Gregor Mendel discovered the laws of inheritance in 1865. Although little known before the end of the century, Mendel's discovery gained great importance in the early 1900s with the birth of the science of genetics. Some time later, the structures of genes and chromosomes were discovered. The discovery, in the 1950s, of the DNA molecule, which incorporates genetic information, threw the theory of evolution into a great crisis, because the origin of the immense amount of information in DNA could not possibly be explained by coincidental happenings.

Besides all these scientific developments, no transitional forms, which were supposed to show the gradual evolution of living organisms from primitive to advanced species, have ever been found despite years of search.

These developments ought to have resulted in Darwin's theory being banished to the dustbin of history. However, it was not, because certain circles insisted on revising, renewing, and elevating the theory to a scientific platform. These efforts gain meaning only if we realise that behind the theory lie ideological intentions rather than scientific concerns.

Nevertheless, some circles that believed in the necessity of upholding a theory that had reached an impasse soon set up a new model. The name of this new model was neo-Darwinism. According to this theory, species evolved as a result of mutations, minor changes in their genes, and the fittest ones survived through the mechanism of natural selection. When, however, it was proved that the mechanisms proposed by neo-Darwinism were invalid and minor changes were not sufficient for the formation of living beings, evolutionists went on to look for new models. They came up with a new claim called "punctuated equilibrium" that rests on no rational or scientific grounds. This model held that living beings suddenly evolved into another species without any transitional forms. In other words, species with no evolutionary "ancestors" suddenly appeared. This was a way of describing creation, though evolutionists would be loath to admit this. They tried to cover it up with incomprehensible scenarios. For instance, they said that the first bird in history could all of a sudden inexplicably have popped out of a reptile egg. The same theory also held that carnivorous land-dwelling animals could have turned

**Charles Darwin**

into giant whales, having undergone a sudden and comprehensive transformation.

These claims, totally contradicting all the rules of genetics, biophysics, and biochemistry are as scientific as fairy-tales of frogs turning into princes! Nevertheless, being distressed by the crisis that the neo-Darwinist assertion was in, some evolutionist paleontologists embraced this theory, which has the distinction of being even more bizarre than neo-Darwinism itself.

The only purpose of this model was to provide an explanation for the gaps in the fossil record that the neo-Darwinist model could not explain. However, it is hardly rational to attempt to explain the gap in the fossil record of the evolution of birds with a claim that "a bird popped all of a sudden out of a reptile egg", because, by the evolutionists' own admission, the evolution of a species to another species requires a great and advantageous change in genetic information. However, no mutation whatsoever improves the genetic information or adds new information to it. Mutations only derange genetic information. Thus, the "gross mutations" imagined by the punctuated equilibrium model, would only cause "gross", that is "great", reductions and impairments in the genetic information.

The theory of punctuated equilibrium was obviously merely a product of the imagination. Despite this evident truth, the advocates of evolution did not hesitate to honour this theory. The fact that the model of evolution proposed by Darwin could not be proved by the fossil record forced them to do so. Darwin claimed that species underwent a gradual change, which necessitated the existence of half-bird/half-reptile or half-fish/half-reptile freaks. However, not even one of these "transitional forms" was found despite the extensive studies of evolutionists and the hundreds of thousands of fossils that were unearthed.

Evolutionists seized upon the model of punctuated equilibrium with the hope of concealing this great fossil fiasco. As we have stated before, it was very evident that this theory is a fantasy, so it very soon consumed itself. The model of punctuated equilibrium was never put forward as a consistent model, but rather used as an escape in cases that plainly did not fit the model of gradual evolution. Since evolutionists today realise that complex organs such as eyes, wings, lungs, brain and others explicitly refute the model of gradual evolution, in these particular points they are compelled to take shelter in the fantastic interpretations of the model of punctuated equilibrium.

## IS THERE ANY FOSSIL RECORD TO VERIFY THE THEORY OF EVOLUTION?

The theory of evolution argues that the evolution of a species into another species takes place gradually, step-by-step over millions of years. The logical inference drawn from such a claim is that monstrous living organisms called "transitional forms" should have lived during these periods of transformation. Since evolutionists allege that all living things evolved from each other step-by-step, the number and variety of these transitional forms should have been in the millions.

If such creatures had really lived, then we should see their remains everywhere. In fact, if this thesis is correct, the number of intermediate transitional forms should be even greater than the number of animal species alive today and their fossilised remains should be abundant all over the world.

Since Darwin, evolutionists have been searching for fossils and the result has been for them a crushing disappointment. Nowhere in the world – neither on land nor in the depths of the sea – has any intermediate transitional form between any two species ever been uncovered.

Darwin himself was quite aware of the absence of such transitional forms. It was his greatest hope that they would be found in the future. Despite his hopefulness, he saw that the biggest stumbling block to his theory was the missing transitional forms. This is why, in his book *The Origin of Species*, he wrote:

> Why, if species have descended from other species by fine gradations, do we not everywhere see innumerable transitional forms? Why is not all nature in confusion, instead of the species being, as we see them, well defined?... But, as by this theory innumerable transitional forms must have existed, why do we not find them embedded in countless numbers in the crust of the earth?... But in the intermediate region, having intermediate conditions of life, why do

we not now find closely-linking intermediate varieties? This difficulty for a long time quite confounded me.[1]

Darwin was right to be worried. The problem bothered other evolutionists as well. A famous British paleontologist, Derek V. Ager, admits this embarrassing fact:

> The point emerges that if we examine the fossil record in detail, whether at the level of orders or of species, we find – over and over again – not gradual evolution, but the sudden explosion of one group at the expense of another.[2]

The gaps in the fossil record cannot be explained away by the wishful thinking that not enough fossils have yet been unearthed and that these missing fossils will one day be found. Another evolutionist paleontologist, T. Neville George, explains the reason:

> There is no need to apologise any longer for the poverty of the fossil record. In some ways, it has become almost unmanageably rich and discovery is outpacing integration... The fossil record nevertheless continues to be composed mainly of gaps.[3]

## LIFE EMERGED ON EARTH SUDDENLY AND IN COMPLEX FORMS

When terrestrial strata and the fossil record are examined, it is seen that living organisms appeared simultaneously. The oldest stratum of the earth in which fossils of living creatures have been found is that of the "Cambrian", which has an estimated age of 530-520 million years.

Living creatures that are found in the strata belonging to the Cambrian period emerged in the fossil record all of a sudden without any pre-existing ancestors. The vast mosaic of living organisms, made up of such great numbers of complex creatures, emerged so suddenly that this miraculous event is referred to as the "Cambrian Explosion" in scientific literature.

Most of the organisms found in this stratum have highly advanced organs like eyes, or systems seen in organisms with a highly advanced organisation such as gills, circulatory systems, and so on. There is no sign in the fossil record to indicate that these organisms had any ancestors. Richard Monestarsky, the editor of *Earth Sciences* magazine, states about

A 320-million-year-old cockroach fossil (left). A 360-million-year-old trilobite fossil (below).

the sudden emergence of living species:

> A half-billion years ago the remarkably complex forms of animals that we see today suddenly appeared. This moment, right at the start of Earth's Cambrian Period, some 550 million years ago, marks the evolutionary explosion that filled the seas with the world's first complex creatures. The large animal phyla of today were present already in the early Cambrian and they were as distinct from each other then as they are today.[4]

Not being able to find answers to the question of how earth came to overflow with thousands of different animal species, evolutionists posit an imaginary period of 20 million years before the Cambrian Period to explain how life originated and "the unknown happened". This period is called the "evolutionary gap". No evidence for it has ever been found and the concept is still conveniently nebulous and undefined even today.

In 1984, numerous complex invertebrates were unearthed in

*Allah is Known Through Reason*

## The Most Cherished Pieces of Evidence of Evolution are Proven to be Invalid

A four hundred and ten million-year-old Coelacanth fish fossil (below). Evolutionists claimed that it was the transitional form proving the transition of this fish from water to land. The fact that more than forty living examples of this fish have been caught in the last fifty years reveals that this is still a perfectly ordinary fish and that it is still living. A one hundred and thirty-five million-year-old Archaeopteryx fossil, the alleged ancestor of birds, which is said to have evolved from dinosaurs (left). Research on the fossil showed it, on the contrary, to be an extinct bird that had once flown but later lost that ability.

Chengjiang, set in the central Yunnan plateau in the high country of southwest China. Among them were trilobites, now extinct, but no less complex in structure than any modern invertebrate.

The Swedish evolutionist paleontologist, Stefan Bengston, explains the situation as follows:

> If any event in life's history resembles man's creation myths, it is this sudden diversification of marine life when multicellular organisms took over as the dominant actors in ecology and evolution. Baffling (and embarrassing) to Darwin, this event still dazzles us.[5]

The sudden appearance of these complex living beings with no predecessors is no less baffling (and embarrassing) for evolutionists today than it was for Darwin 135 years ago. In nearly a century and a half, they have advanced not one step beyond the point that stymied Darwin.

As may be seen, the fossil record indicates that living things did not evolve from primitive to advanced forms, but instead emerged all of a sudden and in a perfect state. The absence of the transitional forms is not peculiar to the Cambrian period. Not a single transitional form verifying the alleged evolutionary "progression" of vertebrates – from fish to amphibians, reptiles, birds, and mammals – has ever been found. Every living species appears instantaneously and in its current form, perfect and complete, in the fossil record.

In other words, living beings did not come into existence through evolution. They were created.

## EVOLUTION FORGERIES
### Deceptions in Drawings

The fossil record is the principal source for those who seek evidence for the theory of evolution. When inspected carefully and without prejudice, the fossil record refutes the theory of evolution rather than supporting it. Nevertheless, misleading interpretations of fossils by evolutionists and their prejudiced representation to the public have given many people the impression that the fossil record indeed supports the theory of evolution.

The susceptibility of some findings in the fossil record to all kinds of interpretations is what best serves the evolutionists' purposes. The fossils unearthed are most of the time unsatisfactory for reliable identification. They usually consist of scattered, incomplete bone fragments. For this reason, it is very easy to distort the available data and to use it as desired. Not surprisingly, the reconstructions (drawings and models) made by evolutionists based on such fossil remains are prepared entirely speculatively in order to confirm evolutionary theses. Since people are readily affected by visual information, these imaginary reconstructed models are employed to convince them that the reconstructed creatures really existed in the past.

Evolutionist researchers draw human-like imaginary creatures, usually setting out from a single tooth, or a mandible fragment or a humerus, and present them to the public in a sensational manner as if they were links in human evolution. These drawings have played a great role in the estab-

Continuously running into such skilfully drawn half-man half-ape creatures in books or other publications, the public becomes convinced that man evolved from the ape or some similar creature. These drawings, however, are outright forgeries.

lishment of the image of "primitive men" in the minds of many people.

These studies based on bone remains can only reveal very general characteristics of the creature concerned. The distinctive details are present in the soft tissues that quickly vanish with time. With the soft tissues speculatively interpreted, everything becomes possible within the boundaries of the imagination of the reconstruction's producer. Earnst A. Hooten from Harvard University explains the situation like this:

> To attempt to restore the soft parts is an even more hazardous undertaking. The lips, the eyes, the ears, and the nasal tip leave no clues on the underlying bony parts. You can with equal facility model on a Neanderthaloid skull the features of a chimpanzee or the lineaments of a philosopher. These alleged restorations of ancient types of man have very little if any scientific value and are likely only to mislead the public... So put not your trust in reconstructions.[6]

### Studies Made to Fabricate False Fossils

Unable to find valid evidence in the fossil record for the theory of evolution, some evolutionists have ventured to manufacture their own. These efforts, which have even been included in encyclopaedias under the heading "evolution forgeries", are the most telling indication that the theory of evolution is an ideology and a philosophy that evolutionists are hard put to defend. Two of the most egregious and notorious of these forgeries are described below.

**Piltdown Man**

Charles Dawson, a well-known doctor and amateur paleoanthropologist, came forth with a claim that he had found a jawbone and a cranial fragment in a pit in the area of Piltdown, England, in 1912. Although the skull was human-like, the jawbone was distinctly simian. These specimens were christened the "Piltdown Man". Alleged to be 500 thousand years old, they were displayed as absolute proofs of human evolution. For more than 40 years, many scientific articles were written on the "Piltdown Man", many interpretations and drawings were made and the fossil was presented as crucial evidence of human evolution.

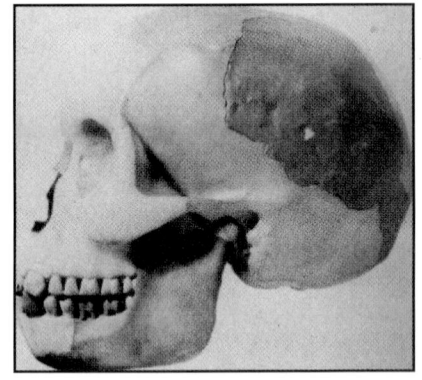

False fossil: Piltdown Man

In 1949, scientists examined the fossil once more and concluded that the "fossil" was a deliberate forgery consisting of a human skull and the jawbone of an orang-utan.

Using the fluorine dating method, investigators discovered that the skull was only a few thousand years old. The teeth in the jawbone, which belonged to an orang-utan, had been artificially worn down and the "primitive" tools that had conveniently accompanied the fossils were crude forgeries that had been sharpened with steel implements. In the detailed analysis completed by Oakley, Weiner and Clark, they revealed this forgery to the public in 1953. The skull belonged to a 500-year-old man, and the mandibular bone belonged to a recently deceased ape! The teeth were thereafter specially arranged in an array and added to the jaw and the joints were filed in order to make them resemble that of a man. Then all these pieces were stained with potassium dichromate to give them a dated appearance. (These stains disappeared when dipped in acid.) Le Gros Clark, who was a member of the team that disclosed the forgery, could not hide his astonishment:

> The evidences of artificial abrasion immediately sprang to the eye. Indeed so obvious did they seem it may well be asked: how was it that they had escaped notice before? [7]

### Nebraska Man

In 1922, Henry Fairfield Osborn, the director of the American Museum of Natural History, declared that he had found a molar tooth fossil in western Nebraska near Snake Brook belonging to the Pliocene period. This tooth allegedly bore the common characteristics of both man and ape. Deep scientific arguments began in which some interpreted this tooth to

The above picture was drawn based on a single tooth and it was published in the Illustrated London News of 24th July 1922. However, evolutionists were extremely disappointed when it was revealed that this tooth belonged neither to an ape-like creature nor to a man, but to an extinct species of pig.

*Evolution Deceit* 111

be that of Pithecanthropus erectus while others claimed it was closer to that of modern human beings. This fossil, which aroused extensive debate, was popularly named "Nebraska Man". It was also immediately given a "scientific name": "Hesperopithecus Haroldcooki".

Many authorities gave Osborn their support. Based on this single tooth, reconstructions of Nebraska Man's head and body were drawn. Moreover, Nebraska Man was even pictured with a whole family.

In 1927, other parts of the skeleton were also found. According to these newly discovered pieces, the tooth belonged neither to a man nor to an ape. It was realised that it belonged to an extinct species of wild American pig called Prosthennops.

## DID MEN AND APES COME FROM A COMMON ANCESTOR?

According to the claims of the theory of evolution, men and modern apes have common ancestors. These creatures evolved in time and some of them became the apes of today, while another group that followed another branch of evolution became the men of today.

Evolutionists call the so-called first common ancestors of men and apes "Australopithecus" which means "South African ape". Australopithecus, nothing but an old ape species that has become extinct, has various types. Some of them are robust, while others are small and slight.

Evolutionists classify the next stage of human evolution as "Homo", that is "man". According to the evolutionist claim, the living beings in the Homo series are more developed than Australopithecus, and not very much different from modern man. The modern man of our day, Homo sapiens, is said to have formed at the latest stage of the evolution of this species.

The fact of the matter is that the beings called Australopithecus in this imaginary scenario fabricated by evolutionists really are apes that became extinct, and the beings in the Homo series are members of various human races that lived in the past and then disappeared. Evolutionists arranged various ape and human fossils in an order from the smallest to the biggest in order to form a "human evolution" scheme. Research, however, has demonstrated that these fossils by no means imply an evolutionary process and some of these alleged ancestors of man were real apes whereas some of them were real humans.

Now, let us have a look at Australopithecus, which represents to evolutionists the first stage of the scheme of human evolution.

### Australopithecus: Extinct Apes

Evolutionists claim that Australopithecus are the most primitive ancestors of modern men. These are an old species with a head and skull structure similar to that of modern apes, yet with a smaller cranial capacity. According to the claims of evolutionists, these creatures have a very important feature that authenticates them as the ancestors of men: bipedalism.

The movements of apes and men are completely different. Human beings are the only living creatures that move freely about on two feet. Some other animals do have a limited ability to move in this way, but those that do have bent skeletons.

According to evolutionists, these living beings called Australopithecus had the ability to walk in a bent rather than an upright posture like human beings. Even this limited bipedal stride was sufficient to encourage evolutionists to project onto these creatures that they were the ancestors of man.

However, the first evidence refuting the allegations of evolutionists that Australopithecus were bipedal came from evolutionists themselves. Detailed studies made on Australopithecus fossils forced even evolutionists to admit that these looked "too" ape-like. Having conducted detailed anatomical research on Australopithecus fossils in the mid-1970s, Charles E. Oxnard likened the skeletal structure of Australopithecus to that of modern orang-utans:

> An important part of today's conventional wisdom about human evolution is based on studies of teeth, jaws and skull fragments of australopithecine fossils. These all indicate that the close relation of the australopithecine to the human lineage may not be true. All these fossils are different from gorillas, chimpanzees and men. Studied as a group, the australopithecine seems more like the orang-utan. [8]

What really embarrassed evolutionists was the discovery that

Australopithecus could not have walked on two feet and with a bent posture. It would have been physically very ineffective for Australopithecus, allegedly bipedal but with a bent stride, to move about in such a way because of the enormous energy demands it would have entailed. By means of computer simulations conducted in 1996, the English paleoanthropologist Robin Crompton also demonstrated that such a "compound" stride was impossible. Crompton reached the following conclusion: a living being can walk either upright or on all fours. A type of in-between stride cannot be sustained for long periods because of the extreme energy consumption. This means that Australopithecus could not have been both bipedal and have a bent walking posture.

Probably the most important study demonstrating that Australopithecus could not have been bipedal came in 1994 from the research anatomist Fred Spoor and his team in the Department of Human Anatomy and Cellular Biology at the University of Liverpool, England. This group conducted studies on the bipedalism of fossilised living beings. Their research investigated the involuntary balance mechanism found in the cochlea of the ear, and the findings showed conclusively that Australopithecus could not have been bipedal. This precluded any claims that Australopithecus was human-like.

### The Homo Series: Real Human Beings

The next step in the imaginary human evolution is "Homo", that is, the human series. These living beings are humans who are no different from modern men, yet who have some racial differences. Seeking to exaggerate these differences, evolutionists represent these people not as a "race" of modern man but as a different "species". However, as we will soon see, the people in the Homo series are nothing but ordinary human racial types.

According to the fanciful scheme of evolutionists, the internal imaginary evolution of the Homo species is as follows: First Homo erectus, then Homo sapiens archaic and Neanderthal Man, later Cro-Magnon Man and finally modern man.

Despite the claims of evolutionists to the contrary, all the "species" we have enumerated above are nothing but genuine human beings. Let us first examine Homo erectus, who evolutionists refer to as the most primitive human species.

The most striking evidence showing that Homo erectus is not a "primitive" species is the fossil of "Turkana Boy", one of the oldest Homo erectus remains. It is estimated that the fossil was of a 12-year-old boy, who would have been 1.83 meters tall in his adolescence. The upright skeletal structure of the fossil is no different from that of modern man. Its tall and slender skeletal structure totally complies with that of the people living in tropical regions in our day. This fossil is one of the most important pieces of evidence that Homo erectus is simply another specimen of the modern human race. Evolutionist paleontologist Richard Leakey compares Homo erectus and modern man as follows:

> One would also see differences in the shape of the skull, in the degree of protrusion of the face, the robustness of the brows and so on. These differences are probably no more pronounced than we see today between the separate geographical races of modern humans. Such biological variation arises when populations are geographically separated from each other for significant lengths of time.[9]

Leakey means to say that the difference between Homo erectus and us is no more than the difference between Negroes and Eskimos. The cranial features of Homo erectus resulted from their manner of feeding, and genetic emigration and from their not assimilating with other human races for a lengthy period.

Another strong piece of evidence that Homo erectus is not a "primitive" species is that fossils of this species have been unearthed aged twenty-seven thousand years and even thirteen thousand years. According to an article published in *Time* – which is not a scientific periodical, but nevertheless had a sweeping effect on the world of science – Homo erectus fossils aged twenty-seven thousand years were found on the island of Java. In the Kow swamp in Australia, some thirteen thousand year-old fossils were found that bore Homo Sapiens-Homo Erectus characteristics. All these fossils demonstrate that Homo erectus continued living up to times very close to our day and were nothing but a human race that has since been buried in history.

### Archaic Homo Sapiens and Neanderthal Man

Archaic Homo sapiens is the immediate forerunner of contemporary man in the imaginary evolutionary scheme. In fact, evolutionists do not have much to say about these men, as there are only minor differences between them and modern men. Some researchers even state that representatives of this race are still living today, and point to the Aborigines in Australia as an example. Like Homo sapiens, the Aborigines also have thick protruding eyebrows, an inward-inclined mandibular structure, and a slightly smaller cranial volume. Moreover, significant discoveries have been made hinting that such people lived in Hungary and in some villages in Italy until not very long ago.

Evolutionists point to human fossils unearthed in the Neander valley of Holland which have been named Neanderthal Man. Many contemporary researchers define Neanderthal Man as a sub-species of modern man and call it "Homo sapiens neandertalensis". It is definite that this race lived together with modern humans, at the same time and in the same areas. The findings testify that Neanderthals buried their dead, fashioned musical instruments, and had cultural affinities with the Homo sapiens sapiens living during the same period. Entirely modern skulls and skeletal structures of Neanderthal fossils are not open to any speculation. A prominent authority on the subject, Erik Trinkaus from New Mexico University writes:

> Detailed comparisons of Neanderthal skeletal remains with those of modern humans have shown that there is nothing in Neanderthal anatomy that conclusively indicates locomotor, manipulative, intellectual, or linguistic abilities inferior to those of modern humans.[10]

In fact, Neanderthals even had some "evolutionary" advantages over modern men. The cranial capacity of Neanderthals was larger than that of the modern man and they were more robust and muscular than we are. Trinkaus adds: "One of the most characteristic features of the Neanderthals is the exaggerated massiveness of their trunk and limb bones. All of the preserved bones suggest a strength seldom attained by modern humans.

Furthermore, not only is this robustness present among the adult males, as one might expect, but it is also evident in the adult females, adolescents, and even children."

To put it precisely, Neanderthals are a particular human race that assimilated with other races in time.

All of these factors show that the scenario of "human evolution" fabricated by evolutionists is a figment of their imaginations, and that men have always been men and apes always apes.

## CAN LIFE RESULT FROM COINCIDENCES AS EVOLUTION ARGUES?

The theory of evolution holds that life started with a cell that formed by chance under primitive earth conditions. Let us therefore examine the composition of the cell with simple comparisons in order to show how irrational it is to ascribe the existence of the cell – a structure which still maintains its mystery in many respects, even at a time when we are about to set foot in the 21st century – to natural phenomena and coincidences.

With all its operational systems, systems of communication, transportation and management, a cell is no less complex than any city. It contains power stations producing the energy consumed by the cell, factories manufacturing the enzymes and hormones essential for life, a databank where all necessary information about all products to be produced is recorded, complex transportation systems and pipelines for carrying raw materials and products from one place to another, advanced laboratories and refineries for breaking down imported raw materials into their usable parts, and specialised cell membrane proteins for the control of incoming and outgoing materials. These constitute only a small part of this incredibly complex system.

Far from being formed under primitive earth conditions, the cell, which in its composition and mechanisms is so complex, cannot be synthesised in even the most sophisticated laboratories of our day. Even with the use of amino acids, the building blocks of the cell, it is not possible to produce so much as a single organelle of the cell, such as mitochondria or ribosome, much less a whole cell. The first cell claimed to have been produced by evolutionary coincidence is as much a figment of the imagination and a product of fantasy as the unicorn.

## Proteins Challenge Coincidence

And it is not just the cell that cannot be produced: the formation, under natural conditions, of even a single protein of the thousands of complex protein molecules making up a cell is impossible.

Proteins are giant molecules consisting of amino acids arranged in a particular sequence in certain quantities and structures. These molecules constitute the building blocks of a living cell. The simplest is composed of 50 amino acids; but there are some proteins that are composed of thousands of amino acids. The absence, addition, or replacement of a single amino acid in the structure of a protein in living cells, each of which has a particular function, causes the protein to become a useless molecular heap. Incapable of demonstrating the "accidental formation" of amino acids, the theory of evolution founders on the point of the formation of proteins.

We can easily demonstrate, with simple probability calculations anybody can understand, that the functional structure of proteins can by no means come about by chance.

There are twenty different amino acids. If we consider that an average-sized protein molecule is composed of 288 amino acids, there are $10^{300}$ different combinations of acids. Of all of these possible sequences, only "one" forms the desired protein molecule. The other amino-acid chains are either completely useless or else potentially harmful to living things. In other words, the probability of the coincidental formation of only one protein molecule cited above is "1 in $10^{300}$". The probability of this "1" occurring out of an "astronomical" number consisting of 1 followed by 300 zeros is for all practical purposes zero; it is impossible. Furthermore, a protein molecule of 288 amino acids is rather a modest one compared with some giant protein molecules consisting of thousands of amino acids. When we apply similar probability calculations to these giant protein molecules, we see that even the word "impossible" becomes inadequate.

If the coincidental formation of even one of these proteins is impossible, it is billions of times more impossible for approximately one million of those proteins to come together by chance in an organised fashion and make up a complete human cell. Moreover, a cell is not merely a collection of proteins. In addition to proteins, cells also include nucleic acids, carbohydrates, lipids, vitamins, and many other chemicals such as electrolytes, all of which are arranged harmoniously and with design in specific proportions, both in terms of structure and function. Each functions as a building block or component in various organelles.

As we have seen, evolution is unable to explain the formation of even a single protein out of the millions in the cell, let alone explain the cell.

Prof. Dr. Ali Demirsoy, one of the foremost authorities of evolutionist thought in Turkey, in his book *Kalitim ve Evrim* (Inheritance and Evolution), discusses the probability of the accidental formation of Cytochrome-C, one of the essential enzymes for life:

> The probability of the formation of a Cytochrome-C sequence is as likely as zero. That is, if life requires a certain sequence, it can be said that this has a probability likely to be realised once in the whole universe. Otherwise, some metaphysical powers beyond our definition should have acted in its formation. To accept the latter is not appropriate to the goals of science. We therefore have to look into the first hypothesis.[11]

After these lines, Demirsoy admits that this probability, which he accepted just because it was "more appropriate to the goals of science", is unrealistic:

> The probability of providing the particular amino acid sequence of Cytochrome-C is as unlikely as the possibility of a monkey writing the history of humanity on a typewriter – taking it for granted that the monkey pushes the keys at random.[12]

The correct sequence of proper amino acids is simply not enough for the formation of one of the protein molecules present in living things. Besides this, each of the twenty different types of amino acid present in the composition of proteins must be left-handed. Chemically, there are two different types of amino acids called "left-handed" and "right-handed". The difference between them is the mirror-symmetry between their three dimensional structures, which is similar to that of a person's right and left hands. Amino acids of either of these two types are found in equal numbers in nature and they can bond perfectly well with one another. Yet, research uncovers an astonishing fact: all proteins present in the structure of living things are made up of left-handed amino acids. Even a single right-handed amino acid attached to the structure of a protein renders it useless.

Let us for an instant suppose that life came into existence by chance as evolutionists claim. In this case, the right and left-handed amino acids that were generated by chance should be present in nature in roughly equal amounts. The question of how proteins can pick out only left-handed amino acids, and how not even a single right-handed amino acid becomes involved in the life process is something that still confounds evolutionists. In the *Britannica Science Encyclopaedia*, an ardent defender of evolution, the authors indicate that the amino acids of all living organisms on earth and the building blocks of complex polymers such as proteins have the same left-handed asymmetry. They add that this is tantamount to tossing a coin a million times and always getting heads. In the same encyclopaedia, they state that it is not possible to understand why molecules become left-handed or right-handed and that this choice is fascinatingly related to the source of life on earth.[13]

It is not enough for amino acids to be arranged in the correct numbers, sequences, and in the required three-dimensional structures. The formation of a protein also requires that amino acid molecules with more than one arm be linked to each other only through certain arms. Such a bond is called a "peptide bond". Amino acids can make different bonds with each other; but proteins comprise those and only those amino acids that join together by "peptide" bonds.

Research has shown that only 50 % of amino acids, combining at random, combine with a peptide bond and that the rest combine with different bonds that are not present in proteins. To function properly, each amino acid making up a protein must join with other amino acids with a peptide bond, as it has only to be chosen from among the left-handed ones. Unquestionably, there is no control mechanism to select and leave out the right-handed amino acids and personally make sure that each amino acid makes a peptide bond with the other.

Under these circumstances, the probabilities of an average protein molecule comprising five hundred amino acids arranging itself in the correct quantities and in sequence, in addition to the probabilities of all of the amino acids it contains being only left-handed and combining using only peptide bonds are as follows:

- The probability of being in the right sequence = $1/20^{500}$ = $1/10^{650}$
- The probability of being left-handed = $1/2^{500}$ = $1/10^{150}$
- The probability of combining using a "peptide bond" = $1/2^{499}$ = $1/10^{150}$

TOTAL PROBABILITY = $1/10^{950}$ that is, **"1" probability in $10^{950}$**

As you can see above, the probability of the formation of a protein molecule comprising five hundred amino acids is "1" divided by a number formed by placing 950 zeros after a 1, a number incomprehensible to the human mind. This is only a probability on paper. Practically, such a possibility has "0" chance of realisation. In mathematics, a probability smaller than 1 over $10^{50}$ is statistically considered to have a "0" probability of realisation.

While the improbability of the formation of a protein molecule made up of five hundred amino acids reaches such an extent, we can further proceed to push the limits of the mind to higher levels of improbability. In the "haemoglobin" molecule, a vital protein, there are five hundred and seventy-four amino acids, which is a much larger number than that of the amino acids making up the protein mentioned above. Now consider this: in only one out of the billions of red blood cells in your body, there are "280,000,000" (280 million) haemoglobin molecules. The supposed age of the earth is not sufficient to afford the formation of even a single protein, let alone a red blood cell, by the method of "trial and error". The conclusion from all this is that evolution falls into a terrible abyss of improbability right at the stage of the formation of a single protein.

The probability of an average protein molecule comprising five hundred amino acids being arranged in the correct proportion and sequence in addition to the probability of all of the amino acids it contains being only left-handed and being combined only with peptide bonds is "1" divided by 10950. We can write this number, which is formed by putting 950 zeros after 1, as follows:

$$10^{950} =$$

100,000,000,000,000,000,000,000,000,000,000,000,000,000,000,000,000,000,000,000,000,000,000,000,000,000,000,000,000,000,000,000,000,000,000,000,000,000,000,000,000,000,000,000,000,000,000,000,000,000,000,000,000,000,000,000,000,000,000,000,000,000,000,000,000,000,000,000,000,000,000,000,000,000,000,000,000,000,000,000,000,000,000,000,000,000,000,000,000,000,000,000,000,000,000,000,000,000,000,000,000,000,000,000,000,000,000,000,000,000,000,000,000,000,000,000,000,000,000,000,000,000,000,000,000,000,000,000,000,000,000,000,000,000,000,000,000,000,000,000,000,000,000,000,000,000,000,000,000,000,000,000,000,000,000,000,000,000,000,000,000,000,000,000,000,000,000,000,000,000,000,000,000,000,000,000,000,000,000,000,000,000,000,000,000,000,000,000,000,000,000,000,000,000,000,000,000,000,000,000,000,000,000,000,000,000,000,000,000,000,000,000,000,000,000,000,000,000,000,000,000,000,000,000,000,000,000,000,000,000,000,000,000,000,000,000,000,000,000,000,000,000,000,000,000,000,000,000,000,000,000,000,000,000,000,000,000,000,000,000,000,000,000,000,000,000,000,000,000,000,000,000,000,000,000,000,000,000,000,000,000,000,000,000,000,000,000,000,000,000,000,000,000,000,000,000,000,000,000,000,000,000,000,000,000,000,000,000,000,000,000

### Looking for Answers to the Generation of Life

Well aware of the terrible odds against the possibility of life forming by chance, evolutionists were unable to provide a rational explanation for their beliefs, so they set about looking for ways to demonstrate that the odds were not so unfavourable.

They designed a number of laboratory experiments to address the question of how life could generate itself from non-living matter. The best known and most respected of these experiments is the one known as the "Miller Experiment" or "Urey-Miller Experiment", which was conducted by the American researcher Stanley Miller in 1953.

With the purpose of proving that amino acids could have come into existence by accident, Miller created an atmosphere in his laboratory that he assumed would have existed on primordial earth (but which later proved to be unrealistic) and he set to work. The mixture he used for this primordial atmosphere was composed of ammonia, methane, hydrogen, and water vapour.

Miller knew that methane, ammonia, water vapour and hydrogen would not react with each other under natural conditions. He was aware that he had to inject energy into the mixture to start a reaction. He suggested that this energy could have come from lightning flashes in the primordial atmosphere and, relying on this supposition, he used an artificial electricity discharge in his experiments.

Miller boiled this gas mixture at 100 $^0$C for a week, and, in addition, he introduced an electric current into the chamber. At the end of the week, Miller analysed the chemicals that had been formed in the chamber and observed that three of the twenty amino acids, which constitute the basic elements of proteins, had been synthesised.

This experiment aroused great excitement among evolutionists and they promoted it as an outstanding success. Encouraged by the thought that this experiment definitely verified their theory, evolutionists immediately produced new scenarios. Miller had supposedly proved that amino acids could form by themselves. Relying on this, they hurriedly hypothesised the following stages. According to their scenario, amino acids had later by accident united in the proper sequences to form proteins. Some of these accidentally formed proteins placed themselves in cell membrane-like structures, which "somehow" came into existence and formed a primitive cell. The cells united in time and formed living organisms. The greatest mainstay of the scenario was Miller's experiment.

However, Miller's experiment was nothing but make-believe, and has since been proven invalid in many respects.

### The Invalidity of Miller's Experiment

Nearly half a century has passed since Miller conducted his experiment. Although it has been shown to be invalid in many respects, evolutionists still advance Miller and his results as absolute proof that life could have formed spontaneously from non-living matter. When we assess Miller's experiment critically, without the bias and subjectivity of evolutionist thinking, however, it is evident that the situation is not as rosy as evolutionists would have us think. Miller set for himself the goal of proving that amino acids could form by themselves in earth's primitive conditions. Some amino acids were produced, but the conduct of the experiment conflicts with his goal in many ways, as we shall now see.

✦ Miller isolated the amino acids from the environment as soon as they were formed, by using a mechanism called a "cold trap". Had he not done so, the conditions of the environment in which the amino acids formed would immediately have destroyed the molecules.

It is quite meaningless to suppose that some conscious mechanism of this sort was integral to earth's primordial conditions, which involved ultraviolet radiation, thunderbolts, various chemicals, and a high percentage of free oxygen. Without such a mechanism, any amino acid that did manage to form would immediately have been destroyed.

✦ The primordial atmospheric environment that Miller attempted to simulate in his experiment was not realistic. Nitrogen and carbon dioxide would have been constituents of the primordial atmosphere, but Miller disregarded this and used methane and ammonia instead.

Why? Why were evolutionists insistent on the point that the primitive atmosphere contained high amounts of methane ($CH_4$), ammonia ($NH_3$), and water vapour ($H_2O$)? The answer is simple: without ammonia, it is impossible to synthesise an amino acid. Kevin McKean talks about this in an article published in *Discover* magazine:

> Miller and Urey imitated the ancient atmosphere of earth with a mixture of methane and ammonia. According to them, the earth was a true homogeneous mixture of metal, rock and ice. However in the latest studies, it is understood that the earth was very hot at those times and that it was composed of melted nickel and iron. Therefore, the chemical atmosphere of that time should have been formed mostly of nitrogen ($N_2$), carbon dioxide ($CO_2$) and water vapour ($H_2O$). However these are not as appropriate as methane and ammonia for the production of organic molecules.[14]

After a long period of silence, Miller himself also confessed that the atmospheric environment he used in his experiment was not realistic.

✦ Another important point invalidating Miller's experiment is that there was enough oxygen to destroy all the amino acids in the atmosphere at the time when evolutionists thought that amino acids formed. This oxygen concentration would definitely have hindered the formation of amino acids. This situation completely negates Miller's experiment, in which he totally neglected oxygen. If he had used oxygen in the experiment, methane would have decomposed into carbon dioxide and water, and ammonia would have decomposed into nitrogen and water.

On the other hand, since no ozone layer yet existed, no organic molecule could possibly have lived on earth because it was entirely unprotected against intense ultraviolet rays.

✦ In addition to a few amino acids essential for life, Miller's experiment also produced many organic acids with characteristics that are quite detrimental to the structures and functions of living things. If he had not isolated the amino acids and had left them in the same environment with these chemicals, their destruction or transformation into different compounds through chemical reactions would have been unavoidable. Moreover, a large number of right-handed amino acids also formed. The existence of these amino acids alone refuted the theory, even within its own reasoning, because right-handed amino acids are unable to function in the composition of living organisms and render proteins useless when they are involved in their composition.

To conclude, the circumstances in which amino acids formed in Miller's experiment were not suitable for life forms to come into being. The medium in which they formed was an acidic mixture that destroyed and oxidised any useful molecules that might have been obtained.

Evolutionists themselves actually refute the theory of evolution, as they are often wont to do, by advancing this experiment as "proof". If the experiment proves anything, it is that amino acids can only be produced in a controlled laboratory environment where all the necessary conditions have been specifically and consciously designed. That is, the experiment shows that what brings life (even the "near-life" of amino acids) into being cannot be unconscious chance, but rather conscious will – in a word, Creation.

This is why every stage of Creation is a sign proving to us the existence and might of Allah.

## The Miraculous Molecule: DNA

The theory of evolution has been unable to provide a coherent explanation for the existence of the molecules that are the basis of the cell. Furthermore, developments in the science of genetics and the discovery of the nucleic acids (DNA and RNA) have produced brand-new problems for the theory of evolution.

In 1955, the work of two scientists on DNA, James Watson and Francis Crick, launched a new era in biology. Many scientists directed their attention to the science of genetics. Today, after years of research, scientists have, largely, mapped the structure of DNA.

Here, we need to give some very basic information on the structure and function of DNA:

The molecule called DNA, which exists in the nucleus of each of the 100 trillion cells in our body, contains the complete construction plan of the human body. Information regarding all the characteristics of a person, from the physical appearance to the structure of the inner organs, is recorded in DNA by means of a special coding system. The information in DNA is coded within the sequence of four special bases that make up this molecule. These bases are specified as A, T, G, and C according to the initial letters of their names. All the structural differences among people depend on the variations in the sequence of these bases. There are approximately 3.5 billion nucleotides, that is, 3.5 billion letters in a DNA molecule.

The DNA data pertaining to a particular organ or protein is included in special components called "genes". For instance, information about the eye exists in a series of special genes, whereas information about the heart exists in quite another series of genes. The cell produces proteins by using the information in all of these genes. Amino acids that constitute the structure of the protein are defined by the sequential arrangement of three nucleotides in the DNA.

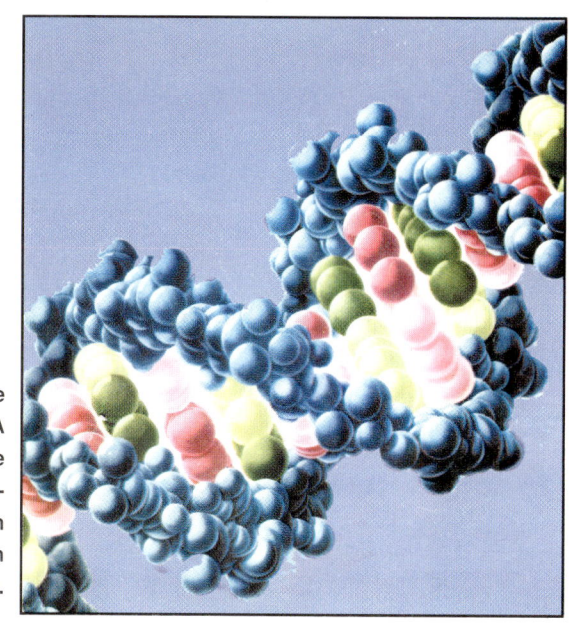

**The molecule called DNA contains the complete construction plan of the human body.**

At this point, an important detail deserves attention. An error in the sequence of nucleotides making up a gene renders the gene completely useless. When we consider that there are 200 thousand genes in the human body, it becomes more evident how impossible it is for the millions of nucleotides making up these genes to form by accident in the right sequence. An evolutionist biologist, Frank Salisbury, comments on this impossibility by saying:

> A medium protein might include about 300 amino acids. The DNA gene controlling this would have about 1,000 nucleotides in its chain. Since there are four kinds of nucleotides in a DNA chain, one consisting of 1,000 links could exist in $4^{1000}$ forms. Using a little algebra (logarithms), we can see that $4^{1000}=10^{600}$. Ten multiplied by itself 600 times gives the figure 1 followed by 600 zeros! This number is completely beyond our comprehension.[15]

The number $4^{1000}$ is equivalent to $10^{600}$. We obtain this number by adding 600 zeros to 1. As 10 with 11 zeros indicates a trillion, a figure with 600 zeros is indeed a number that is difficult to grasp.

Evolutionist Prof. Ali Demirsoy was forced to make the following admission on this issue:

> In fact, the probability of the random formation of a protein and a nucleic acid (DNA-RNA) is inconceivably small. The chances against the emergence of even a particular protein chain are astronomic.[16]

*Evolution Deceit*

In addition to all these improbabilities, DNA can barely be involved in a reaction because of its double-chained spiral shape. This also makes it impossible to think that it can be the basis of life.

Moreover, while DNA can replicate only with the help of some enzymes that are actually proteins, the synthesis of these enzymes can be realised only by the information coded in DNA. As they both depend on each other, either they have to exist at the same time for replication, or one of them has had to be "created" before the other. American microbiologist Jacobson comments on the subject:

> The complete directions for the reproduction of plans, for energy and the extraction of parts from the current environment, for the growth sequence, and for the effector mechanism translating instructions into growth – all had to be simultaneously present at that moment (when life began). This combination of events has seemed an incredibly unlikely happenstance, and has often been ascribed to divine intervention.[17]

The quotation above was written two years after the disclosure of the structure of DNA by James Watson and Francis Crick. Despite all the developments in science, this problem remains unsolved for evolutionists. To sum up, the need for DNA in reproduction, the necessity of the presence of some proteins for reproduction, and the requirement to produce these proteins according to the information in the DNA entirely demolish evolutionist theses.

Two German scientists, Junker and Scherer, explained that the synthesis of each of the molecules required for chemical evolution, necessitates distinct conditions, and that the probability of the compounding of these materials having theoretically very different acquirement methods is zero:

> Until now, no experiment is known in which we can obtain all the molecules necessary for chemical evolution. Therefore, it is essential to produce various molecules in different places under very suitable conditions and then to carry them to another place for reaction by protecting them from harmful elements like hydrolysis and photolysis.[18]

In short, the theory of evolution is unable to prove any of the evolutionary stages that allegedly occur at the molecular level.

To summarise what we have said so far, neither amino acids nor their products, the proteins making up the cells of living beings, could ever be produced in any so-called "primitive atmosphere" environment. Moreover, factors such as the incredibly complex structure of proteins, their right-hand, left-hand features, and the difficulties in the formation of peptide bonds are just parts of the reason why they will never be produced in any future experiment either.

Even if we suppose for a moment that proteins somehow did form accidentally, that would still have no meaning, for proteins are nothing at all on their own: they cannot themselves reproduce. Protein synthesis is only possible with the information coded in DNA and RNA molecules. Without DNA and RNA, it is impossible for a protein to reproduce. The specific sequence of the twenty different amino acids encoded in DNA determines the structure of each protein in the body. However, as has been made abundantly clear by all those who have studied these molecules, it is impossible for DNA and RNA to form by chance.

## THE FACT OF CREATION

With the collapse of the theory of evolution in every field, prominent names in the discipline of microbiology today admit the fact of creation and have begun to defend the view that everything is created by a conscious Creator as part of an exalted creation. This is already a fact that people cannot disregard. Scientists who can approach their work with an open mind have developed a view called "intelligent design". Michael J. Behe, one of the foremost of these scientists, states that he accepts the absolute being of the Creator and describes the impasse of those who deny this fact:

> The result of these cumulative efforts to investigate the cell – to investigate life at the molecular level – is a loud, clear, piercing cry of "design!" The result is so unambiguous and so significant that it must be ranked as one of the greatest achievements in the history of science. This triumph of science should evoke cries of "Eureka" from ten thousand throats.
>
> But, no bottles have been uncorked, no hands clapped. Instead, a curious, embarrassed silence surrounds the stark complexity of the cell. When the subject comes up in public, feet start to shuffle, and breathing gets a bit laboured. In private people are a bit more relaxed; many explicitly admit the

obvious but then stare at the ground, shake their heads, and let it go like that. Why does the scientific community not greedily embrace its startling discovery? Why is the observation of design handled with intellectual gloves? The dilemma is that while one side of the elephant is labelled intelligent design, the other side must be labelled God.[19]

Today, many people are not even aware that they are in a position of accepting a body of fallacy as truth in the name of science, instead of believing in Allah. Those who do not find the sentence "Allah created you from nothing" scientific enough can believe that the first living being came into being by thunderbolts striking a "primordial soup" billions of years ago.

As we have described elsewhere in this book, the balances in nature are so delicate and so numerous that it is entirely irrational to claim that they developed "by chance". No matter how much those who cannot set themselves free from this irrationality may strive, the signs of Allah in the heavens and the earth are completely obvious and they are undeniable.

Allah is the Creator of the heavens, the earth and all that is in between. The signs of His being have encompassed the entire universe.

# Philosophies that made the Mistake of Denying Allah

In previous chapters we saw the clear signs of the existence of Allah. Unquestionably, what we have described here is only a very small portion of His infinite evidence. Wherever one turns, one comes across signs that point to the existence of the Creator.

Well, then, why are there still so many atheists in the world? Furthermore, why is it that some scientists are still atheists? Why do they insist on denying the existence of Allah, despite so many obvious signs?

When we look for answers to these questions, we come across a number of philosophical prejudices which shape the beliefs of atheistic people–including those of atheist scientists. Generally defined as materialism, this philosophical view holds that the universe is eternal and operates without any need for a Creator. According to atheists, matter is the only power that exists. Matter is not created and it functions in an uncontrolled fashion without the intervention of a Creator. There are many philosophers in history who have held this view. Many, from the adherents of the pagan religions of ancient Sumer to the atomistic philosophers of ancient Greece and the dialectical materialists of modern times, have denied the existence of Allah on the strength of this view.

Their denials, however, rest on no solid ground. They have simply convinced themselves about the eternity of matter and have strongly embraced this belief. They have accepted the theory of evolution with the same reasoning and persevered in their belief. And as the famous American microbiologist Michael Behe once noted, when confronted by the realisation that life is too complex to have ever originated by chance, they can only keep silent and change the subject.

This situation shows that there exist prejudices that cause these people to commit themselves to materialism, and its natural outcome, atheism. Their denial of the existence of Allah comes not of evaluating concrete facts from an objective point of view, but rather in spite of those concrete facts.

Moreover, they try to impose their denial on the public at large.

## AUTHORS OF "EVIL PLOTS"

The organised propaganda against faith in Allah indicates that these movements are manipulated from specific centres. In other words, there are a number of power centres that make a considerable effort to break down the religious beliefs of the community. Not surprisingly, Allah has called attention to these groups in the Qur'an. In one verse, a group of people punished by hell-fire in the hereafter call out to their leaders who have led them astray in the world, and say:

> Nay! it was a plot (of yours) by day and by night: Behold! You (constantly) ordered us to be ungrateful to Allah and to attribute equals to Him! (Surah Saba, 33)

These groups who, by hatching evil plots, order others to be ungrateful to Allah have made an appearance in every period of history under different names and guises. Their basic characteristics have nonetheless always been the same. Allah has described them in the Qur'an as "the luxurious ones" (Surat al-Mumenoon, 64) or "the leaders of the arrogant party among their people" (Surat al-Araf, 75), which means that these people are those who are supremely privileged in material terms, who enjoy prestige in society and who display arrogance and haughtiness because of their possessions. Regarding religion as a threat to the concessions they have snatched with injustice and oppression, they want to eliminate it. This is why they fabricate "evil plots" in order to lead their community to apostasy.

Of course there cannot be a single definition of such organised powers. They assume different identities and forms in different societies. When, however, we take a look at the history of the last three or four centuries, we come across an international organisation that answers to the description in the Qur'an.

That organisation is freemasonry.

At this point we also need to stress that the global struggle of freemasonry is undertaken and supported by a power centre that is mentioned in the Qur'an: Jewry. Although Judaism is a divine religion and Jews are adherents of that religion, they have played, as we have mentioned above, a crucial role in anti-religious propaganda conducted all over the world. This is mainly due to the arbitrary alteration of the Old Testament by rabbis and the insinuation of superstitious beliefs into the pure religion announced by the Prophet Musa. Having ceased to be a divine religion as a result of alterations by Jewish rabbis, Jewry has become a worldly and chauvinist ideology. Ultimately various ultra-conservative Jews, who regard religion as a concept exclusive to themselves, have taken the position that Christianity and Islam are "false religions" that must be abolished. Besides, this interesting interplay makes those in question act as powers that strive to erase all religious beliefs from the world. This is the very logic of the alliance between Jewry and freemasonry.

## THE ROLE OF FREEMASONRY

Having its roots in the Western world, from which it subsequently spread elsewhere, this secret organisation has always been the source of all anti-religionist thought and activity in every country it has infiltrated.

A close investigation of the history of the war against religion fought in any country of the world over the last couple of centuries reveals that freemasonry has always been at the centre of such efforts. The history of Europe is remarkably clear-cut on this point. This is why the leader of the Catholic world, Pope Leo XIII, took particular aim at freemasonry in his famous encyclical *Humanum Genus* (1884), in which he described the objectives of the organisation thus:

> In our time, with the aid and support of an association called freemasonry, which has a wide and strong organisation, the efforts of those who

worship dark powers have been united. These no more feel the necessity of hiding their ill will and fight against the Holy Being of God. All aims and efforts of freemasons lead to one intention: to abolish all social and religious disciplines of Christianity and establish a new system of rules based on the principles of naturalism and their own thoughts.[20]

This papal analysis made at the end of the 19th century is absolutely right. When we review contemporary masonic publications, we see that the basic objective of this organisation is to abolish all religious beliefs in society. A Turkish freemasonry lodge declares in one of its pamphlets how religion will be abolished through "the dissemination of positive sciences to society."

> Finally I want to say the following: The most humanistic and Masonic mission that falls to us is not to divert from positive science and reason, to disseminate this by acknowledging that this is the best and only way for evolution, and tutor the public in the positive sciences. The following words of Ernest Renan are very noteworthy:"If the public is tutored and enlightened in the positive sciences and reason, then the vain beliefs of religions will eventually be dismissed."[21]

Here, what is meant by "positive science" is essentially "positivist science" that is, the materialist philosophy that denies everything that has not been obtained by experiment and observation. The mission of freemasonry, on the other hand, is to impose this philosophy on people in the name of "science" and thus abolish all religious beliefs. The theory of evolution has a very crucial role in this indoctrination campaign, as is also made clear in the quotation above. Freemasonry holds that fostering belief in evolution in society is its greatest task.

This organisational connection is a very important factor underlying the reason why both the theory of evolution and materialist philosophy and its derivatives are so assiduously promoted in all corners of the world. The organisation of freemasonry and its offshoots have played an important role in the systematic propaganda being executed against religious beliefs over the last couple of centuries. This is why the founders of diverse -sometimes even contradictory- philosophical systems that deny the existence of Allah have all been masons.

## MASON PHILOSOPHERS

As we stated above, the founders of anti-religionist philosophical systems are actually part of a methodical war being fought against religion. This is why we discover that most of the philosophers who have founded these systems are part of the organisation of freemasonry, which stands at the centre of the war against religion.

In this context, the philosophers who draw immediate attention are the French intellectuals who were the forerunners of the French Revolution. These people not only criticised religious authorities but also fomented violent antagonism against religion. Among them are Diderot, the author of *The System of Nature*, referred to as the "Bible of Materialism"; Voltaire, who was also an impassioned materialist and opponent of religion; the radical materialist Montesquieu; Jean-Jacques Rousseau, who constructed a new "religion" of his own; and the "Encyclopaedists", all of whom were ardent anti-religionists. The organ of Turkish masons, the magazine *Mimar Sinan*, says of these individuals:

> The 1789 French Revolution was prepared by Mason ideologists. The Declaration of Human Rights that embraces the principles of liberty, equality. and fraternity was written with the inspiration and guidance of our masters such as Montesquieu, Voltaire, Rousseau, and Diderot.[22]

The *Mason Magazine*, also published by Turkish masons notes:

> The pioneers who overthrew the feudal system in France and started the Great Revolution were Montesquieu, Voltaire, J. J. Rousseau, the leading materialist Diderot, and the Encyclopaedists who clustered around him. They were all masons.[23]

The materialistic and anti-religionist ideas that increasingly developed in the years that followed the French Revolution reached their peak in the 19th century. When we look at the leaders of this movement, we again come across freemasonry.

In addition, it is also worth noting that there were many Jews among these figures. This demonstrates that Jews who, in alliance with masons, strive to enfeeble Divine religions such as Christianity and Islam and hold the materialist world view, serve the same purpose on philosophical grounds.

# BEHIND THE SCENES OF SOCIALISM

An eccentric group was founded in Bavaria in southern Germany in 1776. The founder of this group, which called itself the "Illuminati" (that is, "the Enlightened Ones") was a professor of law by the name of Adam Weishaupt. This society is interesting in two respects: it was a very secret society and it had set a very ambitious political program for itself. In the program written by Weishaupt, the two fundamental purposes of the society were identified:

1. The abolition of all monarchies and systematic governments.
2. The abolition of all theistic (divine) religions.

The attitude of the society towards religion was extremely antagonistic. According to the English historian Michael Howard, Weishaupt had a "pathological hatred" for divine religion of any sort.[24]

The society was in fact a sort of Masonic lodge. Weishaupt was a senior freemason and he had organised it along the lines of the traditional organisational style of masonic lodges. The Illuminati grew astonishingly fast. In 1780, with the participation of Baron Von Knigge, one of the greatest masters of the German masonic lodges, the power of the society greatly increased. Weishaupt and Knigge were laying the groundwork for a revolution in Germany that was socialist in everything but name. When the government discovered what they were up to, however, Weishaupt and Knigge found it prudent to disband the society. Its activities were assimilated into their regular freemason lodges. This union took place in 1782.

In the early 1800s, a new society was established in Germany that sought to carry on the Illuminati tradition in Germany. The name of the society was "Society of the Honest Ones". In time, its name was changed to "Society of Communists". The head of this society wanted to create a political program for the group and the first two people they called upon to write the program were two strict communist intellectuals: Karl Marx and Frederick Engels! These two wrote the Communist Manifesto at the instruction of the Society of Communists. One widely-known tenet of the Manifesto was that religion was the "opium of the people" and the tract argued that the elimination of religious beliefs was one of the prerequisites for the ideal of the "classless society", which was posited as humanity's only hope of salvation. It should be noted that both Marx and Engels were of Jewish origin.

The early dominance of masons and Jews in the socialist movement continued in the years that followed. A few of the masons and Jews who championed the socialist movement were:

*Ferdinand Lasalle:* Lasalle, a close friend of Marx, defended the notion of a revolutionist communist dictatorship.

*Victor Adler:* As the right-hand man of Engels, Adler spent considerable effort preaching communism. His son Friedrich Adler became the leader of the Austrian Communist Party.

*Moses Hess:* Born into a conservative Jewish family, Hess was a socialist and a close friend of Marx. He was also a vigorous Zionist. He pioneered the Zionist movement in Europe in his book *Rome and Jerusalem* and laboured to establish a Jewish state in Palestine. He was also an ardent defender of Darwinism all his life.

*Gyorgy Lukacs:* A member of a wealthy Jewish family, Lukacs wrote many books advocating communism. He helped spread communist ideology among young people. He was a leading figure in the revolution that brought communism to power in Hungary.

*Vladimir I. Lenin:* A Jew, just like most of the leaders of the Bolshevik movement in Russia, Lenin became the founder of one of the bloodiest totalitarian regimes in the world.

*Herbert Marcuse:* The son of a Jewish family, Herbert Marcuse re-interpreted Marxism and prepared the grounds for the 1968 student upheaval. He incited leftist college movements that spread all around the world and developed an anarchist ideology that has caused–and still causes—the deaths of numerous young people.

## A PHILOSOPHY AND ITS HIDDEN AGENDA

When we look at the history of philosophy, we see that there are many other atheist and anti-religionist philosophers who are distinguished by virtue of their masonic identity. Among them are thinkers like David

Hume, Holbach, Schelling, John Stuart Mill, Auguste Comte, the Marquis de Sade and sociologists like Emile Durkheim, Ferdinand Tönnies, Herbert Spencer, Sigmund Freud, Henry Bergson and Erich Fromm. All of them are of Jewish origin and all of them strove to turn people away from religion and to establish a social and moral order that was completely irreligious. It should go without saying that Charles Darwin and his views enjoyed a very special position among these figures.

The most important point to note here is that the unbelieving and materialistic philosophies produced by all these thinkers, and by thousands of their like, serve certain political and social interests. As we said at the beginning, the most important reason why people deny Allah is their discomfort with religion, religion being the natural outcome of the belief in Allah. Denying the truth of religion because it conflicts with their interests or with those of the circles they represent, these people have recourse to atheism in order to gain support for themselves.

For this reason, the apparent signs of the existence of Allah are not seen by these people. Or rather, it is not their will that those signs be seen. These people strive greatly to prevent belief in the existence of Allah and they spread this disbelief through society in general. Eventually, masses appear who either do not believe in Allah or else have "forgotten" Him as mentioned in the Qur'an. (Surat at-Tawba, 67)

This is why most people spend their lives without praising Allah at all, thinking that they live independently of Him. However one must not be deceived by this "vain crowd", for Allah has already informed us in the Qur'an that most of mankind does not believe (Surat al-Rad, 1). The following verse also admonishes us about the same subject:

> Were you to follow the common run of those on earth, they will lead you away from the way of Allah. They follow nothing but conjecture: they do nothing but lie. (Surat al-Anaam, 116)

(For detailed information, see: *New Masonic Order* by Harun Yahya)

# The Harms of a Society Model with No Belief in Allah

Allah declares in the Qur'an that He has created mankind according to a certain disposition in the verse: "So set you your face steadily and truly to the Faith: (establish) Allah's handiwork according to the pattern on which He has made mankind." (Surat al-Room, 30). The disposition of mankind relies on being a servant to Allah and having faith in Him. Since man is unable to meet his unlimited wishes and needs by himself, he naturally needs to humble himself before Allah and turn to Him.

If the individual lives in accordance with this disposition, he attains true confidence, peace, happiness and salvation. If he denies this disposition and turns away from Allah, he spends his life in distress, fear, anxiety and grief.

This rule, which is true for man, also holds true for societies. If a society is comprised of people who believe in Allah, it becomes a just, peaceful, happy and wise society. Unquestionably, the opposite also holds true. If a society is unaware of Allah, then the order of such a community is basically ruined, corrupt and primitive.

When societies that have turned away from Allah are examined, this fact is readily seen. One of the most important results of irreligious thought is the abolishment of the concept of morality and the development of completely corrupt societies. Transgressing religious and moral bounds, and catering exclusively to the satisfaction of human wishes, this culture is a system of oppression in the fullest sense of the word. In such a system, all sorts of degeneracies from sexual perversion to drug addiction are encouraged. Eventually, societies that are devoid of human love and are egoistic, ignorant, shallow and nonsensical have grown up.

In a society where people live only for the satisfaction of their own desires, it surely is not possible to maintain peace, love and amity. In such a society, human relations depend on mutual interests. An extreme feeling of distrust prevails. When there is no reason for one to be sincere, honest, reliable or well-behaved, nothing stands in the way of dissimulation, falsehood, or betrayal. The members of such societies have "cast Allah away behind their backs (with contempt)" (Surah Hud, 92) and thus never acknowledged the fear of Allah. Since they cannot "make a just estimate of Allah", they are unmindful of the day of judgement and the day of account. For them, hell is nothing more than an idea appearing in religious books. None of them think that they shall have to give an account of themselves in the presence of Allah after their death for all the sins they have committed during their lives in this world, or that they may ultimately be doomed to an eternal life of torment in hell. Even if they do think about it, they suppose that they will enter paradise after they "pay for their sins", as it is expressed in this verse:

> This because they say 'The Fire shall not touch us but for a few numbered days': For their forgeries deceive them as to their own religion. (Surat Al-e-Imran, 24).

Thus they are led to spend their lives doing their best to satisfy their own desires and needs.

This situation naturally brings on the ethical degeneration and moral collapse that we see in many societies today. In their own reasoning they suppose "we have come into this world but once and will live for only 50-60 years and then die, so let us get the best of things here". The thought system based on this erroneous reasoning may bring with it all kinds of injustice, prostitution, theft, crime and immorality. One subscribing to it may become involved in all kinds of crime, homicide, or fraud. When every individual thinks of nothing but the satisfaction of his own needs and desires, everyone else—including his family and friends—have secondary importance. Other individuals in society have no importance whatsoever.

In a social structure that rests on interest relations to a large degree, the mutual distrust of people hinders the formation of peace both at the social and individual level and it causes people to live permanently in a state of doubt, unease and irresolution. Not knowing by whom, when or how misdeeds will be committed in such a society, people live spiritually in a condition of great fear and distress. General distrust and suspicion cause them to lead very unhappy lives. In a society where all kinds of moral values are disregarded, the outlook of people on notions such as family, honesty and chastity is quite alarming, for they have no fear of Allah.

In such societies, the lives of people do not rely on mutual love and respect. Its members feel no need to show respect to each other. They do not display a caring attitude to each other without a good cause. Actually, they are quite right, in terms of their ignorant reasoning, in behaving this way. They are taught throughout their lives that they have evolved from animals and that their souls will be lost forever upon their death. They therefore deem it meaningless to respect a body of ape origin that will rot under the earth and that they will never see again. In their corrupt logic, "all the others as well as themselves are to die and be buried under the earth, their bodies will decay and their souls will vanish. So why would they bother to do good to other people, and be self-sacrificing?" Indeed, these thoughts permeate the subconscious of everyone who has no belief in Allah or, therefore, in the hereafter. In societies with no belief in Allah, there is no basis for peace, happiness, or confidence.

The purpose of all we have said is not to suggest that "degeneration occurs in societies where there is no belief in Allah, therefore there must be belief in Allah." Allah must be believed in because Allah exists and whoever denies Him commits a great sin before Him. Our intention in noting that societies where belief in Allah does not exist become corrupt is to emphasise that the fundamental viewpoints of these societies are wrong. Wrong viewpoints lead to ill consequences. A society that commits the biggest sin of denying Allah, is sure to suffer the worst outcomes. These outcomes are worthy of attention because they show how mistaken this society is.

The common characteristic of such societies is their being deceived as a whole. As stated in the verse, "Were you to follow the common run of those on earth, they will lead you away from the way of Allah." (Surat al-Anaam, 116), that most of society share a common character creates a "mass" psychology that reinforces the already-existing disbelief. Allah describes such societies that are unmindful of Him and the hereafter as "ignorant" in the Qur'an. Even though the members of this society may study physics, history, biology or similar sciences, they do not have the sense and conscience to acknowledge the power and might of Allah. And they are ignorant in that sense.

Because the members of an ignorant society are not devoted to Allah, they go astray from His path in different ways. They follow people who are incompetent servants of Allah just like themselves, taking them as examples and adhering to their ideas as absolute truths. Ultimately an ignorant society ends up a closed society that increasingly blinds itself, becoming further and further divorced from reason and conscience. As we have stated at the beginning, the most notable aspect of this system is that members of such a society act in consonance with anti-religious indoctrination.

Allah describes in the Qur'an with a striking parable how such a life, resting upon a vain and corrupt basis, is destined to be ruined:

> Which then is best? He that lays his foundation on piety to Allah and His good pleasure? Or he that lays his foundation on an undermined sand-cliff ready to crumble to pieces? And it does crumble to pieces with him, into the fire of hell. And Allah does not guide people that do wrong. (Surat at-Tawba, 109)

There is yet another point to be remembered: every society and every person has the opportunity to be rid of the indoctrination, way of life and philosophy of ignorance. Allah sends them messengers who warn them and inform them of the existence of Allah and the hereafter and who tell them the real meaning of life. And along with His messengers He sends righteous books that answer all the questions that are derived from the very conscience of people. This is the law of Allah that has existed since eternity. In our day, the guide of all people is the Qur'an, which shows the right way and leads people from darkness to light. People will be judged according to their own preferences. The messenger who brought the book to people thus called out to them:

> Say: "O you men! Now Truth has reached you from your Lord! Those who receive guidance, do so for the good of their own souls; those who stray, do so to their own loss: and I am not (set) over you to arrange your affairs. (Surah Yunus, 108)

# The True Promised Home: The Hereafter

It should be evident to anyone with wisdom and conscience that none of the objects that exist, none of the events that transpire, and none of the laws that abide in this universe are either vain or purposeless. The structure and endurance of the universe, as we have shown in previous chapters, are based on very delicate balances. Those balances demonstrate as a matter of unquestionable fact that the universe was CREATED. That being so, can it be said that this universe was created in vain?

Certainly not.

A purpose is sought in even the smallest act committed by someone dwelling on this earth, which does not even occupy as much room as a dust particle among billions of galaxies. So, how reasonable can it be to claim that the entire universe was created in vain?

Allah informs people that they have not been created in vain:

Did you then think that We had created you in jest, and that you would not be brought back to Us (for account)? (Surat al-Mumenoon, 115)

The existence of life on earth is made possible by a train of countless miraculous phenomena extending from the Big Bang to atoms, from atoms to galaxies, and from galaxies to our own planet. Life on earth is such that its every need is subtly planned for and created in the most suitable way: the sun in the sky providing all the needed energy, provisions stored under the ground, and a world furnished everywhere with millions of species of plant and animal varieties. Despite all the extraordinary events we have described, people still can reject the existence of their Creator. Considering it reasonable to be shaped into a man from a sperm, these people do not believe that they will be resurrected after death as informed in the Qur'an, and make irrelevant remarks. Allah has pointed in the Qur'an to the twisted reasoning of the unbelievers and has given them the answer:

> And he makes comparisons for Us, and forgets his own (origin and) Creation: He says, "Who can give life to (dry) bones and decomposed ones (at that)?" Say, "He will give them life Who created them for the first time! for He is well-versed in every kind of creation!" (Surah Ya-Seen, 78-79)

Allah–"He Who created Death and Life"–has created everything in the universe for a specific purpose and thus explained the purpose of man's creation: "that He may try which of you is best in deed: and He is the Exalted in Might, Oft-Forgiving." (Surat al-Mulk, 2) As explained in the verse, this world is a place of trial and, as such, it is temporary. There is an end for all people as well as for the world, the time of which is pre-destined by Allah. People are responsible for living the short-lived lives given to them according to the terms set by Allah and described to them in the Qur'an. In the hereafter they shall have their reward for what they have done here.

## THE EVERLASTING PENALTY

We have described in the course of this book the manifest signs of Allah's existence, the advocates of the system that relies on rejecting Allah, and the kind of social context they seek to establish. Everything that has been discussed so far is concerned with "the life of this world". However, what follows death, that is, the "hereafter" also deserves serious consideration.

Those who labour to advance the systems that rely heavily on disbelief in Allah offer a distressful life to their followers in the world. These people will also cause their adherents to suffer a grievous penalty in the hereafter. There, they will by no means show the close attention they used to show to those foolish people who followed them in the world. On the contrary, there, they will only mind saving themselves as stated in the following verse:

Every soul that has sinned, if it possessed all that is on earth, would fain give it in ransom... (Surah Yunus, 54).

The attitude of those who champion disbelief in the world is also expressed in other verses:

> Every time a new people enters, it curses its sister-people (that went before), until they follow each other, all into the Fire. Says the last about the first: "Our Lord! it is these that misled us: so give them a double penalty in the Fire." He will say: "Doubled for all": but this you do not understand. Then the first will say to the last: "See then! No advantage have you over us; so taste you of the penalty for all that you did! "(Surat al-Araf, 38-39)

As is evident, it does not really make much difference whether one is a member of those who are foremost in disbelief or of those who lag behind. As a result, both groups suffer a great loss and deserve an everlasting penalty for the sins they have committed in the world. In the Qur'an, Allah has described in detail the spirits and the circumstances that these people will have and the penalty they will suffer on the day of resurrection, the day of account, and in hell.

## THE DAY OF RESURRECTION

When Allah mentions the day of resurrection in the Qur'an, He calls it "the day that the caller will call (them) unto something not known..." (Surat al-Qamar, 6) The terror of this day is something that human beings cannot know because they have never encountered anything like it.

Only Allah knows the arrival time of that day. People's learning about this day is limited to what is related in the Qur'an. The day of resurrection will come all of a sudden when nobody expects it.

This day may seize people when they work in their office, sleep at their home, talk on the phone, read a book, laugh, cry or drop their children off at school. Furthermore, this seizure will be so horrifying that no one will have seen anything like it in his lifetime.

The day of resurrection starts with the sounding of the trumpet (Surat al-Muddaththir, 8-10). When this sound is heard all over the world, those who have not used the time given to them by Allah for gaining His good pleasure will be seized by a great fear. Allah describes in the Qur'an the horrifying events that will happen on that day:

> Nay, the hour (of judgement) is the time promised them (for their full recompense): And that hour will be most grievous and most bitter. (Surat al-Qamar, 46)

As the verses relate, the sounding of the trumpet is followed by a great tremor and a roaring so violent as to deafen the ears. In the intensity of this din, the mountains start to shake and slide with the earth beneath them (Surat al-Zalzala, 1-8).

Mountains are crumbled to atoms and become a scattered dust (Surat al-Waqia, 5). At that moment, people very well understand how trivial are the things that they have hitherto cherished. All the material values they have pursued throughout their lives suddenly vanish:

> Therefore, when there comes the great, overwhelming (event),- the day when man shall remember (all) that he strove for, and hell-fire shall be placed in full view for (all) to see. (Surat an-Naziat, 34-36)

On that day, even the mountains made up of stones, earth and rocks are dispersed like carded wool (Surat al-Qaria, 5) Man now becomes aware that this power is not the power of nature. For on that day, nature also is laid low. A tremendous fear and horror rule over all that happens that day. People, animals, and nature are all overwhelmed by this horror. People see that the oceans burst forth (Surat al-Infitar, 3) and that they are set on fire (Surat at-Takwir, 6).

The heavens start shaking just like the earth and they start to be torn away, in a way hitherto unwitnessed. The usual blue colour of the sky that people are accustomed to is transformed and resembles molten brass (Surat al-Maarij, 8). On this day, everything in the sky that used to give light is suddenly darkened; the sun is folded up (Surat at-Takwir, 1), the moon is cleft asunder (Surat al-Qamar, 1), and the sun and the moon are joined together. (Surat al-Qiyama, 9)

Pregnant women lose their children because of the horrifying fear of that day. The fear makes children hoary-headed (Surat al-Muzammil, 17). Children run away from their mothers, women from their husbands, and families from one another. Allah tells the reason in the Qur'an:

> At length, when there comes the deafening noise, that day shall a man flee from his own brother, and from his mother and his father, and from his wife and his children. Each one of them, that day, will have enough concern (of his own) to make him indifferent to the others. (Surah Abasa, 33-37)

## THE DAY OF ACCOUNT

After all the events have taken place on the day of resurrection as described above, the "trumpet" is sounded for the second time. This sound is the outset of the day on which everyone will be resurrected. That day the earth becomes thick with people who are raised up from their graves where they were perhaps buried hundreds and thousands of years ago. The resurrection of people on that day and the state of perplexity they will be in are revealed by the Qur'an:

> The trumpet is sounded, when behold! from the sepulchres (men) rush forth to their Lord! They say: "Ah! Woe unto us! Who has raised us up from our beds of repose?"... (A voice will say:) "This is what (Allah) Most Gracious had promised. And true was the word of the messengers!" It is no more than a single blast, when they are all brought up before Us! Then, on that day, not a soul is wronged in the least, and you are but repaid the meets of your past deeds. (Surah Ya-Seen, 51-54)

On that day, all the things that people declined to think about, that they were not willing to understand, and that they fled from are laid bare. They no longer have any means of escape or denial.

The moment these people, with the stamp of ignomity on their faces, and heads fallen, emerge from their graves and assemble, the earth shines with light and the book of each one is brought by and by to be given to him.

On this day of meeting, when enormous throngs of people hitherto unseen come together, the conditions of the believers and of the unbelievers are certainly different. In the Qur'an, this is related as follows:

> Then he that will be given his record in his right hand will say: "Ah here!

read you my record! I did really understand that my account would (one day) reach me!" And he will be in a life of bliss. (Surat al-Haaqqa, 19-21)

And he that will be given his record in his left hand, will say: "Ah! Would that my record had not been given to me! And that I had never realised how my account (stood)! Ah! Would that (death) had made an end of me! Of no profit to me has been my wealth! My power has perished from me!" (Surat al-Haaqqa, 25-29)

On this day, not an atom's weight of injustice is done to anyone. Everyone is paid back in full to recompense for his deeds in the world. A day of dire difficulty for unbelievers, this day is the one on which their eternal life in hell becomes certain.

The following verses clearly reveal what awaits, on the Day of Account, those who insisted on denying Allah throughout their lives and who followed the callers of futile intentions at the Day of Accounting:

And the trumpet is blown, and all who are in the heavens and all who are in the earth swoon away, save him whom Allah wills. Then it is blown a second time, and behold them standing waiting! And the earth shines with the light of her Lord, and the book is set up, and the prophets and the witnesses are brought, and it is judged between them with truth, and they are not wronged... And every soul is paid back fully what it has done, and He knows best what they have done. And those who disbelieve are driven unto hell in troops: until, when they arrive, there, its gates will be opened. And its keepers say, "Did not messengers come to you from among yourselves, rehearsing to you the signs of your Lord, and warning you of the meeting of this day of yours?" The answer is: "True". But the decree of punishment has been proved true against the unbelievers!. (To them) is said: "Enter you the gates of hell, to dwell therein: and evil is (this) abode of the arrogant!". (Surat az-Zumar, 68-72)

## HELL

The greatest sin one can commit is to rebel against Allah, the Creator and Giver of Life. Created to be a servant to Allah, man, if he conflicts with the purpose of his creation, naturally deserves a punishment befitting his wrongdoing. Hell is the place where this punishment is administered. Most people spend their whole lives in a kind of intoxication without thinking about this at all. One of the most important reasons for this intoxication is their inability to make a correct assessment of Allah. Many people esteem Allah for his affectionate, merciful and forgiving attributes; they do not feel a deep and heartfelt fear of Allah as they are supposed to. This causes these people to be insensitive to the commands and counsels of Allah. Allah particularly forewarns people in the Qur'an about this danger:

> O mankind! Guard against (the punishment of) your Lord, and fear (the coming of) a day when no father can avail aught for his son, nor a son avail aught for his father. Verily, the promise of Allah is true: let not then this present life deceive you, nor let the chief deceiver deceive you about Allah. (Surah Luqman, 33)

Truly, Allah, Possessor of the most beautiful names and attributes, is affectionate, merciful, and forgiving. However, it must also be remembered that Allah, at the same time, is everlastingly Just, the Subduer of all, and the Compeller; that Allah is close to the believers but remote from idolaters, unbelievers and hypocrites; that He is the Lord of retribution; and that hell is the place where His latter attributes will most perfectly be embodied.

People, for some reason, have superstitious beliefs on this subject. They assume that after they die, they will go to hell to pay for the sins they committed in the world, but will then go on to paradise after their punishment is over and abide there for ever. Allah, however, informs us in the Qur'an that life both in hell and paradise will last eternally and that no one will be released from either unless Allah so wills.

> And they say: "The fire shall not touch us but for a few numbered days:" Say: "Have you taken a promise from Allah, for He never breaks His promise? Or is it that you say of Allah what you do not know?" Nay, those who seek gain in evil, and are girt round by their sins, they are companions of the fire: Therein shall they abide for ever. But those who have faith and work righteousness, they are companions of the garden: therein shall they abide for ever. (Surat al-Baqara, 80-82)

People will there encounter such torments as fire, heat, darkness, smoke, narrowness, blindness, constriction, hunger, thirst, festering water, boiling water, and the poisonous tree of zaqqum. In addition to physically injurious penalties, they will also suffer a great spiritual torment that mounts right to the hearts. (Surat al-Humaza, 5-9). The dreadful torments that people who disregard Allah's existence will undergo in hell are described in detail in the Qur'an. The verses reveal how important this subject is for man. The wrath of hell is so great that it cannot be compared to any distress in this world. Allah describes in the Qur'an this terrible finale that awaits the unbelievers:

> By no means! He will be sure to be thrown into that which breaks to pieces, and what will explain to you that which breaks to pieces? (It is) the fire of (the wrath of) Allah kindled (to a blaze), which mounts (right) to the hearts: It shall be made into a vault over them, in columns outstretched. (Surat al-Humaza, 4-9)

> Some faces, that day, will be humiliated, labouring (hard), weary. entering into the blazing fire, made to drink, of a boiling hot spring. No food will there be for them but a bitter dhari' which will neither nourish nor satisfy hunger. (Surat al-Ghashiya, 2-7)

> For the rejectors we have prepared chains, yokes, and a blazing fire. (Surat al-Insan, 4)

> This is the hell which the sinners deny: In its midst and in the midst of boiling hot water will they wander round! (Surat ar-Rahman, 43-44)

> But those who reject (Allah)—for them will be the fire of hell: No term shall be determined for them, so they should die, nor shall its penalty be lightened for them. Thus do We punish every ungrateful one! Therein will they cry aloud (for assistance): "Our Lord! Bring us out: we shall work righteousness, not the (deeds) we used to do!"–"Did We not give you long enough life so that he that would should receive admonition? and (moreover) the warner came to you. So taste (the fruits of your deeds): for the wrong-doers there is no helper." (Surah Fatir, 36-37)

> Those who will be gathered to hell (prone) on their faces, they will be in an evil plight, and, as to path, most astray. (Surat al-Furqan, 34)

> When it (the blazing fire) sees them from a place far off, they will hear

its fury and its raging sigh. And when they are cast, bound together into a constricted place therein, they will plead for destruction there and then! "This day plead not for a single destruction: plead for destruction oft-repeated!" (Surat al-Furqan, 12-14)

## THE TRUE HOME PROMISED TO THE BELIEVERS: PARADISE

Now no person knows what delights of the eye are kept hidden (in reserve) for them–as a reward for their (good) deeds. (Surat as-Sajda: 17)

Paradise is the place promised to believers for their belief in Allah and for their devotion to Him. Paradise, as described in many verses, is a place enveloped in many kinds of blessings and it is a residence of eternal bliss. Allah awards the believers with paradise as compensation for their deeds in the world.

Paradise is a place where the "Merciful" (the mercy of Whom is exclusively for the believers, the Most Merciful, Who awards those who properly use His blessings with more superior and eternal blessings) attribute of Allah is revealed. Paradise, therefore, is a home of delight that harbours every thing that a person's soul may desire and even more as described in the verses.

In some people's minds, the word "paradise" conjures up rather limited notions, for they suppose paradise to be a place of merely natural beauty, such as a delightful meadow. There is, however, a great difference between this limited notion and the paradise described in the Qur'an.

In the Qur'an, paradise is described as a place containing everything a person may desire:

There will be there all that the souls could desire, all that their eyes could delight in: and you shall abide therein. (Surat az-Zukhruf, 71)

In another verse we are told that in paradise there is even more than what man could want:

There will be for them therein all that they wish, and more besides in Our presence. (Surah Qaf, 35)

In other words, contrary to general belief, paradise has numerous blessings to offer, blessing such as remained unseen by human beings throughout their lives in this world and even unimaginable to them. Believers will be granted eternal life in paradise in return for their obedience to Allah in the life of this world and for their having lived according to His wishes.

The paradise that is promised to the believers is described in various verses:

> But give glad tidings to those who believe and work righteousness, that their portion is gardens, beneath which rivers flow. Every time they are fed with fruits therefrom, they say: "Why, this is what we were fed with before," for they are given things in similitude; and they have therein companions pure (and holy); and they abide therein (for ever). (Surat al-Baqara, 25)

> The righteous (will be) amid gardens and fountains (of clear-flowing water). (Their greeting will be): "Enter you here in peace and security." And We shall remove from their hearts any lurking sense of injury: (they will be) brothers (joyfully) facing each other on thrones. There no sense of fatigue shall touch them, nor shall they (ever) be asked to leave. (Surat al-Hijr, 45-48)

> For them will be gardens of eternity; beneath them rivers will flow; they will be adorned therein with bracelets of gold, and they will wear green garments of fine silk and heavy brocade: They will recline therein on raised thrones. How good the recompense! How beautiful a couch to recline on! (Surat al-Kahf, 31)

> Verily the companions of paradise shall that day have joy in all that they do; They and their associates will be in groves of (cool) shade, reclining on thrones; (Every) fruit (enjoyment) will be there for them; they shall have whatever they call for; "Peace!"–a word (of salutation) from a Lord Most Merciful. (Surah Ya-Seen, 55-58)

> As to the righteous (they will be) in a position of security, among gardens and springs; dressed in fine silk and in rich brocade, they will face each other; so; and We shall join them to fair women with beautiful, big, and lustrous eyes. There can they call for every kind of fruit in peace and security; nor will they there taste death, except the first death; and He

will preserve them from the penalty of the blazing fire, as a bounty from your Lord! that will be the supreme achievement! (Surah ad-Dukhan, 51-57)

But those who believe and work deeds of righteousness–to them shall We give a home in heaven, lofty mansions beneath which flow rivers, to dwell therein for aye; an excellent reward for those, who do (good)! (Surat al-Ankaboot, 58)

## A WARNING TO THOSE WHO WOULD BE SAVED FROM ENDLESS TORMENT

Surely, everyone is free to live as he wishes in this world and to choose the path he wants. Nobody has the right to exercise compulsion over another. Yet, as those who believe in the existence and eternal justice of Allah, it is our solemn duty to warn those people who would reject Allah and who are unaware of their current state and course. Allah has informed us of the seriousness of the state of these people:

Which then is best? –he that lays his foundation on piety to Allah and His good pleasure?– or he that lays his foundation on an undermined sand-cliff ready to crumble to pieces? and it crumbles to pieces with him, into the fire of hell. And Allah does not guide people that do wrong. (Surat at-Tawba, 109)

People who deliberately turn their back on the words of Allah, or who unconsciously reject their own Creator, will have no means of salvation in the hereafter. If they do not repent and be guided to Allah, Who created them, they will suffer the greatest penalties possible. The eternal penalty awaiting them is stated thus in the Qur'an:

But those who reject Our signs, they are the (unhappy) companions of the left hand. On them will be fire vaulted over (all round). (Surat al-Balad, 19-20)

The way of relief from the eternal penalty and to deserve eternal paradise is evident:

To have sincere faith in Allah before it is too late.

To spend one's life seeking His good pleasure.

# WARNING

The chapter you are about to reveals a crucial secret of your life. You should read it very attentively and thoroughly for it concerns a subject that is liable to make fundamental changes in your outlook on the external world. The subject of this chapter is not just a point of view, a different approach, or a traditional or philosophical thought: it is a fact which everyone, believing or unbelieving, must admit and which is also proven by science today.

# A Very Different Approach to Matter

People who conscientiously and wisely contemplate their surroundings realise that everything in the universe – both animate and inanimate – must have been created. The question is "Who is the Creator of all these things?"

It is evident that **"the fact of creation"**, which reveals itself in every aspect of the universe, cannot be an outcome of the universe itself. For example, a bug cannot have created itself. The solar system cannot have created or organised itself. Neither plants, humans, bacteria, erythrocytes (red-blood corpuscles), nor butterflies can have created themselves. Also the possibility that all these could have originated "by chance" is not even imaginable.

We therefore arrive at the following conclusion: Everything that we see has been created, but nothing we see can themselves be "creators". The Creator is different from and superior to all that we see with our eyes, a superior power that is invisible but whose existence and attributes are revealed in everything that exists.

This is the point at which those who deny the existence of Allah demur. These people are conditioned not to believe in His existence unless they see Him with their eyes. These people, who disregard the fact of **"creation"**, are forced to ignore the actuality of "creation" manifest throughout the universe and try to prove that the universe and the living things in it have not been created. Evolutionary theory is an essential example of their vain endeavours to this end.

The basic mistake of those who deny Allah is shared by many people who do not really deny the existence of Allah but have a wrong perception of Him. They do not deny creation but have superstitious beliefs about "where" Allah is. Most of them think that Allah is up in the "sky". They tacitly imagine that Allah is behind a very distant planet and interferes with "worldly affairs" once in a while, or perhaps does not intervene at all. They imagine that He created the universe and then left it to itself, leaving people to determine their fates for themselves.

Still others have heard that it is written in the Qur'an that Allah is "everywhere" but they cannot conceive what exactly this means. They think that Allah surrounds everything like radio waves or like an invisible, intangible gas.

However, this and other beliefs that are unable to make clear **"where" Allah is** (and maybe because of that deny Him) are all based on a common mistake. They are prejudiced without any grounds for it and so are then moved to wrong opinions of Allah. What is this prejudice?

This prejudice is about the nature and characteristics of matter. We are so conditioned in our suppositions about the existence of matter that we never think whether it does exist or not or whether it is only a shadow. Modern science demolishes this prejudice and discloses a very important and revealing reality. In the following pages, we will try to clarify this great reality to which the Qur'an points.

## THE WORLD OF ELECTRICAL SIGNALS

All the information that we have about the world in which we live is conveyed to us by our five senses. The world we know of consists of what our eyes see, our hands feel, our noses smell, our tongues taste, and our ears hear. We never think that the "external" world could be anything other than that which our senses present to us, as we have been dependent on only those senses since birth.

Modern research in many different fields of science points to a very different understanding and creates serious doubt about our senses and the world that we perceive with them.

The starting-point of this approach is that the notion of an "external world" shaped in our brain is only a response created in our brain by electrical signals. The redness of apples, the hardness of wood and, moreover, your mother, father, family, and everything that you own, your house, job, and the lines of this book, are comprised only of electrical signals.

Frederick Vester explains the point that science has reached on this subject:

> Statements of some scientists posing that **"man is an image**, everything experienced is temporary and deceptive, and **this universe is a shadow"**, seems to be proven by science in our day.[25]

The famous philosopher, George Berkeley commented on the subject as follows:

> We believe in the existence of objects just because we see and touch them, and they are reflected to us by our perceptions. However, our perceptions are only ideas in our mind. Thus, objects we captivate by perceptions are nothing but ideas, and these ideas are essentially in nowhere but our mind... Since all these exist only in the mind, then it means that **we are beguiled by deceptions when we imagine the universe and things to have an existence outside the mind.** So, none of the surrounding things have an existence out of our mind.[26]

In order to clarify the subject, let us consider our sense of sight, which provides us with the most extensive information about the external world.

Stimulations coming from an object are converted into electrical signals and cause effects in the brain. When we "see", we in fact view the effects of these electrical signals in our mind.

*Allah is Known Through Reason*

## HOW DO WE SEE, HEAR, AND TASTE?

The act of seeing is realised progressively. Light clusters (photons) travel from the object to the eye and pass through the lens at the front of the eye where they are refracted and fall upside-down on the retina at the back of the eye. Here, impinging light is turned into electrical signals that are transmitted by neurons to a tiny spot called the centre of vision in the back of the brain. This electrical signal is perceived as an image in this centre in the brain after a series of processes. The act of seeing actually takes place in this tiny spot in the posterior part of the brain, which is **pitch-dark and completely insulated from light**.

Now, let us reconsider this seemingly ordinary and unremarkable process. When we say, "we see", we are in fact seeing the effects of impulses reaching our eyes and induced in our brain, after they are transformed into electrical signals. That is, **when we say, "we see", we are actually observing electrical signals in our mind**.

All the images we view in our lives are formed in our centre of vision, which only comprises a few cubic centimetres of the volume of the brain. Both the book you are now reading and the boundless landscape you see when you gaze at the horizon fit into this tiny space. Another point that has to be kept in mind is that, as we have noted before, the brain is insulated from light; its inside is absolutely dark. The brain has no contact with light itself.

We can explain this interesting situation with an example. Let us suppose that in front of us there is a burning candle. We can sit opposite this candle and watch it at length. However, during this period, our brain never has any direct contact with the original light of the candle. Even as we see the light of the candle, the inside of our brain is completely dark. We watch a colourful and bright world inside our dark brain.

R. L. Gregory gives the following explanation about the miraculous aspects of seeing, something that we take so much for granted:

> We are so familiar with seeing, that it takes a leap of imagination to realise that there are problems to be solved. But consider it. We are given tiny distorted upside-down images in the eyes, and we see separate solid objects in surrounding space. From the patterns of simulation on the retinas we per-

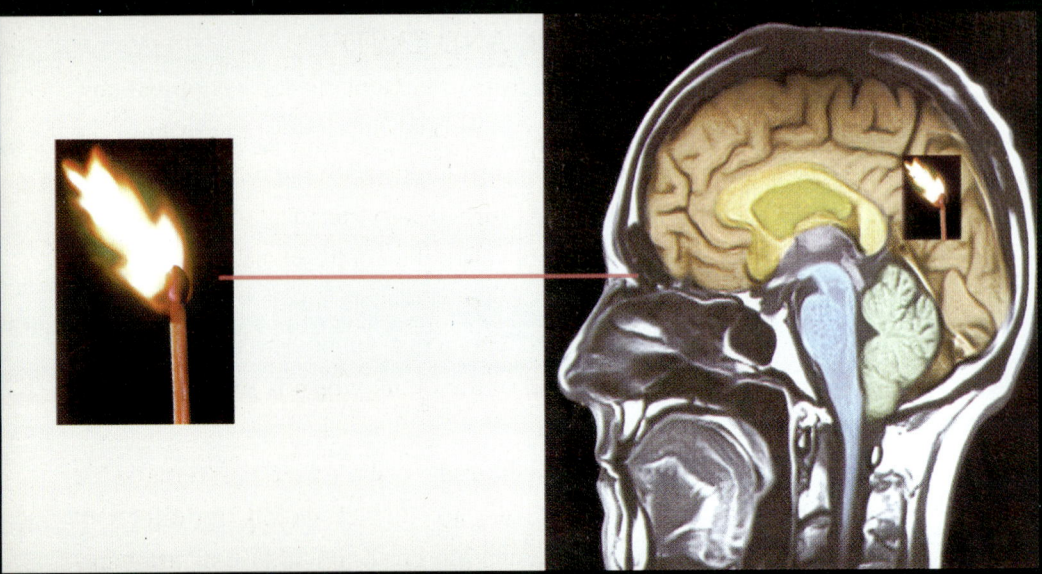

Even at the moment when we feel the light and heat of a fire, the inside of our brain is pitch dark and its temperature never changes.

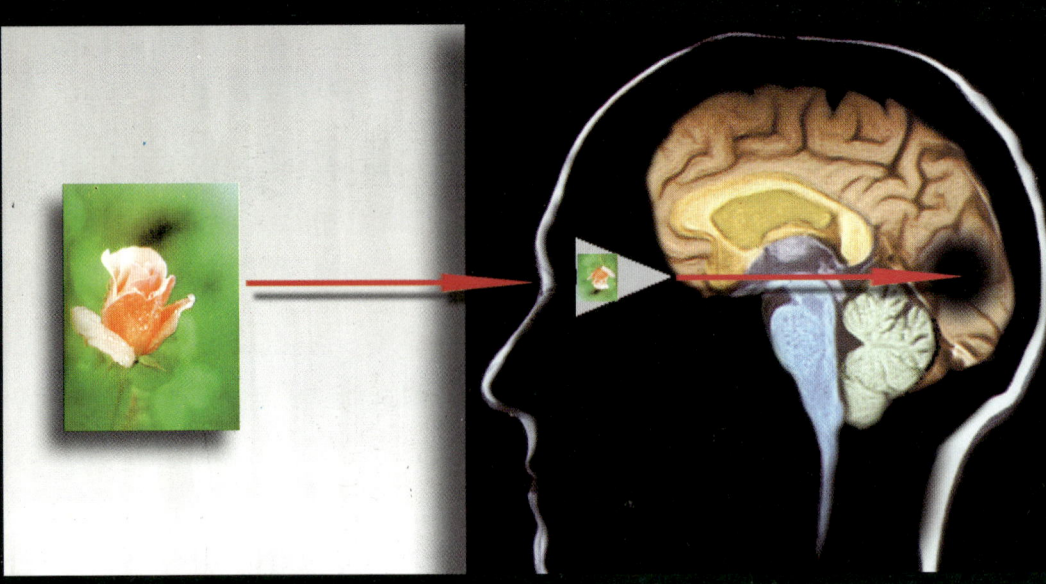

Bundles of light coming from an object falls upside-down on the retina. Here, the image is converted into electrical signals and transmitted to the centre of vision at the back of the brain. Since the brain is insulated from light, it is impossible for light to reach the centre of vision. This means that we view a vast world of light and depth in a tiny spot that is insulated from light.

ceive the world of objects, and **this is nothing short of a miracle.**[27]

The same situation applies to all our other senses. Sound, touch, taste and smell are all transmitted to the brain as electrical signals and are perceived in the relevant centres in the brain.

The sense of hearing works in a similar manner to that of sight. The outer ear picks up sounds by the auricle and directs them to the middle ear. The middle ear transmits the sound vibrations to the inner ear and intensifies them. The inner ear translates the vibrations into electrical signals, which it sends into the brain. Just as with the eye, the act of hearing finally takes place in the centre of hearing in the brain. The brain is insulated from sound just as it is from light. Therefore, no matter how noisy it is outside, the inside of the brain is completely silent.

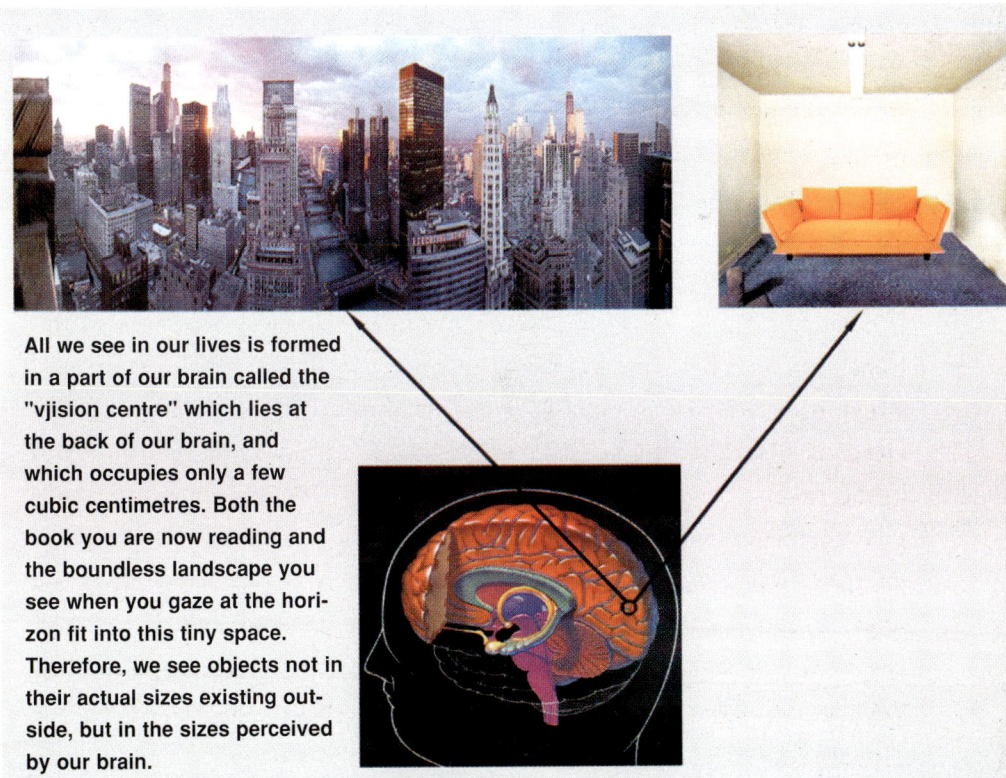

All we see in our lives is formed in a part of our brain called the "vjision centre" which lies at the back of our brain, and which occupies only a few cubic centimetres. Both the book you are now reading and the boundless landscape you see when you gaze at the horizon fit into this tiny space. Therefore, we see objects not in their actual sizes existing outside, but in the sizes perceived by our brain.

*A Very Different Approach to Matter*

Nevertheless, even the subtlest sounds are perceived in the brain. This is so precise that the ear of a healthy person hears everything without any atmospheric noise or interference. In your brain, which is insulated from sound, you listen to the symphonies of an orchestra, hear all the noises of a crowded place, and perceive all the sounds within a wide frequency range, from the rustling of a leaf to the roar of a jet plane. However, if the sound level in your brain were to be measured by a sensitive device at that moment, it would be seen that a complete silence is prevailing there.

Our perception of odour is formed in a similar way. Volatile molecules emitted by things such as vanilla or a rose reach the receptors in the delicate hairs in the epithelium region of the nose and become involved in an interaction. This interaction is transmitted to the brain as electrical signals and perceived as smell. Everything that we smell, be it pleasant or unpleasant, is nothing but the brain's perception of the interactions of volatile molecules after they have been transformed into electrical signals. You perceive the scent of a perfume, a flower, a food that you like, the sea, or other odours you like or dislike, in your brain. The molecules themselves never reach the brain. Just as with sound and vision, what reach your brain simply electrical signals. In other words, all the odours that you have assumed – since you were born – to belong to external objects are just electrical signals that you feel through your sense organs.

Similarly, there are four different types of chemical receptors in the front part of a human's tongue. These pertain to the four tastes: salty, sweet, sour, and bitter. Our taste receptors transform these perceptions into electrical signals through a chain of chemical processes and transmit them to the brain. These signals are perceived as taste by the brain. The taste you experience when you eat a chocolate bar or a fruit that you like is the interpretation of electrical signals by the brain. You can never reach the object in the external world; you can never see, smell or taste the chocolate itself. For instance, if the taste nerves that travel to the brain are cut, the taste of things you eat will not reach your brain; you will completely lose your sense of taste.

At this point, we come across another fact: We can never be sure that what we experience when we taste a food and what another person experiences when he tastes the same food, or what we perceive when we hear a voice and what another person perceives when he hears the same voice are the same. Lincoln Barnett says that no one can know whether another person perceives the colour red or hears the C note the in same way as does he himself.[28]

Our sense of touch is no different from the others. When we touch an object, all information that will help us recognise the external world and objects are transmitted to the brain by the sense nerves on the skin. The feeling of touch is formed in our brain. Contrary to general belief, the place where we perceive the sense of touch is not at our finger-tips or on our skins but at the centre of touch perception in our brains. Because of the brain's interpretation of electrical stimuli coming to it from objects, we experience those objects differently such as that they are hard or soft, hot or cold. We derive all the details that help us recognise an object from these stimuli. Concerning this, the thoughts of two famous philosophers, B. Russell and L. Wittgenstein, are as follows:

> For instance, whether a lemon truly exists or not and how it came to exist cannot be questioned and investigated. A lemon consists merely of a taste sensed by the tongue, an odour sensed by the nose, a colour and shape sensed by the eye; and only these features of it can be subject to examination and assessment. Science can never know the physical world.[29]

It is impossible for us to reach the physical world. All objects around us are a collection of perceptions such as seeing, hearing, and touching. By processing the data in the centre of vision and in other sensory centres, our brains, throughout our lives, **do not confront the "original" of the matter existing outside us but rather the copy formed inside our brain.** It is at this point that we are misled by assuming these copies are instances of real matter outside us.

## "THE EXTERNAL WORLD" INSIDE OUR BRAIN

From the physical facts described so far, we may conclude the following. Everything we see, touch, hear, and perceive as "matter", "the world" or "the universe" is only electrical signals occurring in our brain.

Someone eating a fruit does not confront the actual fruit but its perception in the brain. The object considered by the person a "fruit" actually consists of electrical impressions of the shape, taste, smell, and texture of the fruit in the brain. If the sight nerves travelling to the brain were to be severed suddenly, the image of the fruit would suddenly disappear. A disconnection in the nerve travelling from the sensors in the nose to the brain would completely interrupt the sense of smell. Put simply, the fruit is nothing but the brain's interpretation of electrical signals.

Another point to be considered is **the sense of distance**. Distance, for example the distance between you and this book, is only a feeling of space formed in your brain. Objects that seem to be distant in one person's view also exist in the brain. For instance, someone who watches the stars in the sky assumes that they are millions of light-years away from him. Yet, what he "sees" are really the stars inside himself, in his centre of vision. While you read these lines, you are, in truth, not inside the room you assume yourself to be in; on the contrary, the room is inside you. Your seeing your body makes you think that you are inside it. **However, you must remember that your body, too, is an image formed inside your brain.**

The same applies to all your other perceptions. For instance, when you think that you hear the sound of the television in the next room, you are

**As a result of artificial stimuli, a physical world as true and realistic as the real one can be formed in our brain without the existence of physical world. As a result of artificial stimuli, a person may imaginethink that he is driving in his car, while he is actually sitting at home.**

actually experiencing the sound inside your brain. You can prove neither that a room exists next to yours, nor that a sound comes from the television in that room. Both the sound you think to be coming from metres away and the conversation of a person right next to you are perceived in a centre of hearing a few centimetres square in your brain. Apart from in this centre of perception, no concept such as right, left, front or behind exists. That is, sound does not come to you from the right, from the left or from the air; **there is no direction from which sound comes.**

The smells that you perceive are like that too; none of them reaches you from a great distance. You suppose that the end-effects formed in your centre of smell are the smell of the objects in the external world. However, just as the image of a rose is in your centre of vision, so the smell of the rose is in your centre of smell; there is neither a rose nor an odour pertaining to it in the external world.

The "external world" presented to us by our perceptions is merely a collection of electrical signals reaching our brains. Throughout our lives, our brains process these signals and we live without recognising that we are mistaken in assuming that these are the original versions of things existing in the "external world". We are misled because we can never reach the matters themselves by means of our senses.

Moreover, again our brains interpret and attribute meaning to signals that we assume to be the "external world". For example, let us consider the sense of hearing. Our brains transform the sound waves in the "external world" into a symphony. That is to say, music is also a perception created by our brains. In the same manner, when we see colours, what reach our eyes are merely electrical signals of **different wavelengths**. Again our brains transform these signals into colours. **There are no colours in the "external world".** Neither is the apple red, nor is the sky blue, nor the trees green. They are as they are just because we perceive them to be so **The "external world" depends entirely on the perceiver.**

Even the slightest defect in the retina of the eye causes colour blindness. Some people perceive blue as green, some red as blue, and some perceive all colours as different tones of grey. At this point, it does not mat-

The findings of modern physics show that the universe is a collection of perceptions. The following question appears on the cover of the well-known American science magazine *New Scientist*, which dealt with this matter in its 30 January 1999 issue: "Beyond Reality: Is the Universe Really a Frolic of Primal Information and Matter Just a Mirage?"

ter whether the object externally is coloured or not.

The prominent thinker Berkeley also addressed this fact:

At the beginning, it was believed that **colours, odours**, etc., "really exist", but subsequently such views were renounced, and it was seen that **they only exist in dependence on our sensations.**[30]

In conclusion, the reason we see objects coloured is not because they are coloured or because they have an independent material existence outside ourselves. The truth of the matter is rather that **all the qualities we ascribe to objects are inside us and not in the "external world".**

So what remains of the "external world"?

## IS THE EXISTENCE OF THE "EXTERNAL WORLD" INDISPENSABLE?

So far, we have been speaking repeatedly of an "external world" and a world of perceptions formed in our brains, the latter of which is what we see. However, since we can never actually reach the "external world", how can we be sure that such a world really exists?

Actually we cannot. Since each object is only a collection of perceptions and those perceptions exist only in the mind, it is more accurate to say that **the only world that really exists is the world of perceptions.** The only world we know of is the world that exists in our mind: the one that is designed, recorded, and made vivid there; the one, in short, that is created within our mind. This is the only world of which we can be sure.

We can never prove that the perceptions we observe in our brain have material correlates. Those perceptions could conceivably be coming from an "artificial" source.

It is possible to observe this. False stimuli can produce an entirely imaginary "material world" in our brain. For example, let us imagine a very developed recording instrument in which all kinds of electrical signals could be recorded. First, let us transmit all the data related to a setting (including body image) to this instrument by transforming them into electrical signals. Second, let us imagine that the brain could survive apart from the body. Finally, let us connect the recording instrument to the brain with electrodes that will function as nerves and send the pre-recorded data to the brain. In this state, you would experience yourself living in this artificially created setting. For instance, you could easily believe that you are driving fast on a highway. It might never become possible to understand that you consist of nothing but your brain. This is because what is needed to form a world within your brain is not the existence of a real world but rather the stimuli. It is perfectly possible that these stimuli could be coming from an artificial source, such as a tape-recorder.

In that connection, distinguished philosopher Bertrand Russell wrote:

> As to the sense of touch when we press the table with our fingers, that is an electric disturbance on the electrons and protons of our fingertips, produced, according to modern physics, by the proximity of the electrons and protons in the table. **If the same disturbance in our finger-tips arose in any other way, we should have the sensations, in spite of there being no table.**[31]

It is indeed very easy for us to be deceived into believing perceptions, without any material correlates, to be real. We often experience this feeling in our dreams, in which we experience events, see people, objects and settings that seem completely real. However, they are all nothing but mere perceptions. There is no basic difference between the dream and the "real world"; both of them are experienced in the brain.

## WHO IS THE PERCEIVER?

As we have related so far, there is no doubt that the world we think we inhabit and that we call the "external world" is perceived inside our brain. However, here arises the question of primary importance. If all physical events that we know are intrinsically perceptions, what about our brain? Since our brains are a part of the physical world just like our arms, legs, or any other objects, it also must be a perception just like all other objects.

An example about dreams will illuminate the subject further. Let us think that we see the dream within our brain in accordance with what has been said so far. In the dream, we will have an imaginary body, an imaginary arm, an imaginary eye, and an imaginary brain. If during our dream, we were asked, "where do you see?" we would answer "I see in my brain". Yet, actually there is not any brain to talk about, but an imaginary head and an imaginary brain. The seer of the images is not the imaginary brain in the dream, but a "being" that is far "superior" to it.

We know that there is no physical distinction between the setting of a dream and the setting we call real life. So when we are asked in the setting we call real life the above question "where do you see", it would be just as meaningless to answer "in my brain" as in the example above. In both conditions, the entity that sees and perceives is not the brain, which is after all only a hunk of meat.

When we analyse the brain, we see that there is nothing in it but lipid and protein molecules, which also exist in other living organisms. This means that within the piece of meat we call our "brain", there is nothing to observe the images, to constitute consciousness, or to create the being we call "myself".

R. L. Gregory refers to a mistake people make in relation to the perception of images in the brain:

> There is a temptation, which must be avoided, to say that the eyes produce pictures in the brain. A picture in the brain suggests the need of some kind of internal eye to see it – but this would need a further eye to see its picture... and so on, in an endless regress of eyes and pictures. This is absurd.[32]

This is the very point that puts materialists, who do not hold anything but matter to be true, in a quandary: to whom belongs "the eye inside" that sees, that perceives what it sees and reacts?

Karl Pribram also focused on this important question, about who the perceiver is, in the world of science and philosophy:

> Since the Greeks, philosophers have been thinking about "the ghost in the machine", "the small man within the small man" etc. **Where is "I", the person who uses his brain? Who is it that realises the act of knowing?** As

Saint Francis of Assisi said: "What we search for is the one that sees".33

Now, think of this: The book in your hand, the room you are in, in brief, all the images in front of you are seen inside your brain. Is it the atoms that see these images? Blind, deaf, unconscious atoms? Why did some atoms acquire this quality whereas some did not? Do our acts of thinking, comprehending, remembering, being delighted, being unhappy, and everything else consist of the electrochemical reactions between these atoms?

When we ponder these questions, we see that there is no sense in looking for will in atoms. It is clear that the being that sees, hears, and feels is a supra-material being. This being is "alive" and it is neither matter nor an image of matter. This being associates with the perceptions in front of it by using the image of our body.

**This being is the "soul".**

The aggregate of perceptions we call the "material world" is a dream observed by this soul. Just as the bodies we possess and the material world we see in our dreams have no reality, the universe we occupy and the bodies we possess also have no material reality.

The real being is the soul. Matter consists merely of perceptions viewed by the soul. The intelligent beings that write and read these lines are not each a heap of atoms and molecules and the chemical reactions between them, but a "soul".

## THE REAL ABSOLUTE BEING

All these facts bring us face to face with a very significant question. If the thing we acknowledge to be the material world is merely comprised of perceptions seen by our soul, then what is the source of these perceptions?

In answering this question, we must consider the following: matter does not have a self-governing existence by itself. Since matter is a perception, it is something "artificial". That is, this perception must have been caused by another power, which means that it must have been created. Moreover, this creation must be continuous. If there were not a continuous and consistent creation, then what we call matter would disappear and be lost. This may be likened to a television on which a picture is displayed as long as the signal continues to be broadcast. So, who makes our soul see the stars, the earth, plants, people, our bodies and all else that we see?

It is very evident that there is a Creator, Who has created the entire material universe, that is, the sum of perceptions, and continues His creation ceaselessly. Since this Creator displays such a magnificent creation, He surely has eternal power and might.

This Creator introduces Himself to us. He has revealed a Book within the universe of sensations He has created and through this Book has described Himself, the universe and the reason of our existence to us.

This Creator is Allah and the name of His book is the Qur'an.

The facts that the heavens and the earth, that is, the universe is not stable, that their presence is only made possible by Allah's creating them and that they will disappear when He ends this creation, are all explained in a verse as follows:

> It is Allah Who sustains the heavens and the earth, lest they cease (to function): and if they should fail, there is none - not one - can sustain them thereafter: Verily He is Most Forbearing, Oft-Forgiving. (Surat al-Fatir: 41)

As we mentioned at the beginning, some people have no genuine understanding of Allah and so they imagine Him as a being present somewhere in the heavens and not really intervening in worldly affairs. The

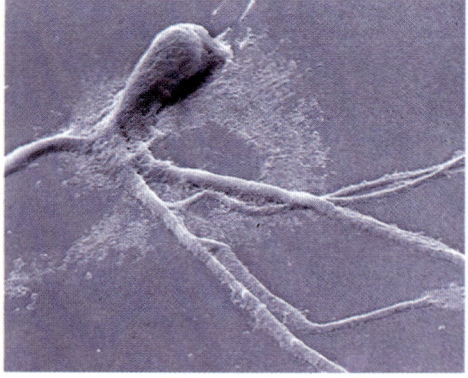

**The brain is a collection of cells made up of protein and fat molecules. It is formed of nerve cells called neurons. There is no power in this piece of meat to observe images, to constitute consciousness, or to create the being we call "myself".**

basis of this logic actually lies in the thought that the universe is an assembly of matter and Allah is "outside" this material world, in a far away place. In some false religions, belief in Allah is limited to this understanding.

However, as we have considered so far, matter is composed only of sensations. And the only real absolute being is Allah. That means that **only Allah is; all things except Him are shadow beings.** Consequently, it is impossible to conceive of Allah as separate and outside of this whole mass of matter. **Allah is surely "everywhere" and encompasses all.** This reality is explained in the Qur'an as follows;

> Allah! There is no god but He, the Living, the Self-subsisting, Eternal. No slumber can seize Him nor sleep. His are all things in the heavens and on earth. Who is there can intercede in His presence except as He permits? He knows what (appears to His creatures as) before or after or behind them. Nor shall they compass aught of His knowledge except as He wills. **His Throne extends over the heavens and the earth,** and He feels no fatigue in guarding and preserving them for He is the Most High, the Supreme (in glory). (Surat al-Baqarah: 255)

That Allah is not bound by space and that He encompasses everything roundabout is stated in another verse as follows:

> To Allah belong the east and the west: **Whithersoever you turn, there is the face of Allah**. For Allah is all-pervading, all-knowing. (Surat al-Baqarah: 115)

Since material beings are each a perception, they cannot see Allah; but Allah sees the matter He created in all its forms. In the Qur'an, this is stated thus: **"No vision can grasp Him, but His grasp is over all vision."** (Surat al-An'am: 103)

That is, we cannot grasp Allah's being with our eyes, but Allah has thoroughly encompassed our inside, outside, looks and thoughts. We cannot utter any word but with His knowledge, nor can we even take a breath.

While we watch these sensory perceptions in the course of our lives, the closest being to us is not any one of these sensations, but Allah Himself. The secret of the following verse in the Qur'an is concealed in this reality: "It is We Who created man, and We know what dark suggestions his soul makes to him: for **We are nearer to him than (his) jugular**

**vein.**" (Surah Qaf: 16) When a person thinks that his body is only made up of "matter", he cannot comprehend this important fact. If he takes his brain to be "himself", then the place that he accepts to be the outside is 20-30 cm away from him. However, when he understands that there is nothing such as matter, and that everything is imagination, notions such as outside, inside, far or near lose meaning. **Allah has encompassed him and He is "infinitely close" to him.**

Allah informs men that He is **"infinitely close"** to them with the verse "When My servants ask you concerning Me, **I am indeed close (to them).**" (Surat al-Baqarah: 186). Another verse relates the same fact: "We told you that **your Lord encompasses mankind round about.**" (Surat al-Isra, 60).

> Why is it not then that when it (soul) comes up to the throat, and you at that time look on, We are nearer to him than you, but you see not. (Surat al-Waqia, 83-85)

Man is misled in thinking that the being closest to him is himself. Allah, in truth, is even closer to us than ourselves. He has called our attention to this point in the verse "Why is it not then that when it (soul) comes up to the throat, and you at that time look on, **We are nearer to him than you, but you see not.**" (Surat al-Waqi'ah: 83-85). As we are told in the verse, people live unaware of this phenomenal fact because they do not see it with their eyes.

On the other hand, it is impossible for man, who is nothing but a shadow being, to have power and will independent of Allah. The verse "But **Allah has created you and what you do!**" (Surat as-Saffat: 96) shows that everything we experience takes place under Allah's control. In the Qur'an, this reality is stated in the verse "**You did not throw, when you threw, it was Allah who threw**" (Surat al-Anfal, 17) whereby it is emphasised that no act is independent of Allah. Since the human being is a shadow being, he himself does not perform the act of throwing. However, Allah gives this shadow being the feeling of self. In reality, Allah performs all acts. If someone takes the acts he does as his own, he evidently means to deceive himself.

This is the reality. A person may not want to concede this and may think of himself as a being independent of Allah; but this does not change a thing. Of course his unwise denial is again within Allah's will and wish.

## EVERYTHING THAT YOU POSSESS IS INTRINSICALLY ILLUSORY

As may be seen clearly, it is a logical scientific fact that the "external world" has no material reality and that it is a collection of images perpetually presented to our soul by Allah. Nevertheless, people usually do not include, or rather do not want to include, everything in the concept of the "external world".

Think about this issue sincerely and boldly. You will realise that your house, furniture, car – which is perhaps recently bought, office, jewellery, bank account, wardrobe, spouse, children, colleagues, and everything else that you possess are in fact included in this imaginary external world projected to you. Everything you see, hear, or smell – in short – perceive with your five senses around you is a part of this "imaginary world": the voice of your favourite singer, the hardness of the chair you sit on, a perfume whose smell you like, the sun that keeps you warm, a flower with beautiful colours, a bird flying in front of your window, a speedboat moving swiftly on the water, your fertile garden, the computer you use at your job, or your hi-fi that has the most advanced technology in the world...

This is the reality, because the world is only a collection of images created to test man. People are tested all through their limited lives with perceptions having no reality. These perceptions are intentionally presented as appealing and attractive. This fact is mentioned in the Qur'an:

> Fair in the eyes of people is the love of things they covet: Women and sons; heaped-up hoards of gold and silver; horses branded (for blood and excellence); and (wealth of) cattle and well-tilled land. Such are the possessions of this world's life; but in nearness to Allah is the best of the goals (to return to). (Surat Ali 'Imran: 14)

Most people cast their religion away for the lure of property, wealth, heaped-up hoards of gold and silver, dollars, jewellery, bank accounts, credit cards, wardrobes full of clothes, last-model cars, in short, all the

If one ponders deeply on all that is said here, one will soon realise this amazing, extraordinary situation by oneself: that all the events in the world are but mere imagination...

forms of prosperity that they either possess or strive to possess. They concentrate only on this world while forgetting the hereafter. They are deceived by the "fair and alluring" face of the life of this world, and fail to keep up prayer, give charity to the poor, and perform worship that will make them prosper in the hereafter. They say instead, "I have things to do", "I have ideals", "I have responsibilities", "I do not have enough time", "I have things to complete" and "I will do it in the future". They consume their lives trying to prosper only in this world. In the verse, **"They know but the outer (things) in the life of this world: but of the End of things they are heedless"** (Surat ar-Rum: 7), this misconception is described.

The fact we describe in this chapter, namely that everything is an image, is very important for its implications that render all lusts and boundaries meaningless. The verification of this fact makes it clear that everything people possess or toil to possess – wealth acquired with greed, children of whom they boast, spouses whom they consider closest to them, friends, their dearest bodies, the social status which they believe to be a superiority, the schools they have attended, the holidays on which they have been – is nothing but mere illusion. Therefore, all the effort, the time spent, and the greed, prove unavailing.

This is why some people unwittingly make fools of themselves when they boast of their wealth and properties or of their "yachts, helicopters, factories, holdings, manors and lands" as if they really exist. Those well-to-do people who ostentatiously sail in their yachts, show off their cars, keep talking about their wealth, suppose that their posts rank them higher than everyone else and keep thinking that they are successful because of all this, should actually think what kind of a state they will find themselves in once they realise that success is nothing but an illusion.

These scenes are seen many times in dreams as well. In their dreams, they also have houses, fast cars, extremely precious jewels, rolls of dollars, and loads of gold and silver. In their dreams, they are also positioned in high ranks, own factories with thousands of workers, possess power to rule over many people, and dress in clothes that make everyone admire them. Just as someone who, on waking, boasted about his possessions in his dreams would be ridiculed, he is sure to be equally ridiculed for boasting of images he sees in this world. Both what he sees in his dreams and in this world are mere images in his mind.

Similarly, the way people react to events they experience in the world will make them feel ashamed when they realise the reality. Those who fiercely fight with each other, rave furiously, swindle, take bribes, commit forgery, lie, covetously withhold their money, do wrong to people, beat and curse others, rage aggressively, are full of passion for office and rank, are envious, and show off, will be disgraced when they realise that they have done all of this in a dream.

Since Allah creates all these images, the Ultimate Owner of everything is Allah alone. This fact is stressed in the Qur'an:

> But to Allah belong all things in the heavens and on earth: And He it is that encompasses all things. (Surat an-Nisa: 126)

It is great foolishness to cast religion away for the sake of imaginary passions and thus lose the eternal life which is meant to be an everlasting deprivation.

At this stage, one point should be understood. It is not said here that "the possessions, wealth, children, spouses, friends, rank you have with which you are being stingy, will vanish sooner or later, and therefore they do not have any meaning", but that "all the possessions you seem to have do not exist, but they are merely dreams composed of images which Allah shows you to test you". As you see, there is a big difference between the two statements.

Although one does not want to acknowledge this right away and would rather deceive oneself by assuming everything one has truly exists, one is finally to die and in the hereafter everything will be clear when we are recreated. On that day **"sharp is one's sight"** (Surah Qaf: 22) and we will see everything much more clearly. However, if we have spent our lives chasing after imaginary aims, we are going to wish we had never lived this life and say "Ah! Would that (Death) had made an end of me! Of no profit to me has been my wealth! My power has perished from me!" (Surat al-Haqqah: 27-29)

What a wise man should do, on the other hand, is to try to understand the greatest reality of the universe here in this world, while he still has time. Otherwise, he will spend all his life running after dreams and face a grievous penalty at the end. In the Qur'an, the final state of those people who run after illusions (or mirages) in this world and forget their Creator, is stated as follows:

> **But the unbelievers, their deeds are like a mirage in sandy deserts,** which the man parched with thirst mistakes for water; until when he comes up to it, he finds it to be nothing: But he finds Allah (ever) with him, and Allah will pay him his account: and Allah is swift in taking account. (Surat an-Nur: 39)

## LOGICAL DEFECTS OF THE MATERIALISTS

From the beginning of this chapter, it is clearly stated that matter does not have absolute being, as materialists claim, but is rather a collection of sense impressions created by Allah. Materialists resist this evident reality, which destroys their philosophy, in an extremely dogmatic manner and bring forward baseless anti-theses.

For example, one of the biggest advocates of materialist philosophy in the 20th century, an ardent Marxist, **George Politzer**, gave the "**bus example**" as the "greatest evidence" for the existence of matter. According to Politzer, philosophers who think that matter is only a perception also run away when they see a bus about to run them over and this is the proof of the physical existence of matter.[34]

When another famous materialist, Johnson, was told that matter is a collection of perceptions, he tried to "prove" the physical existence of stones by giving them a kick.[35]

A similar example is given by **Friedrich Engels**, the mentor of Politzer and founder, along with Marx, of dialectical materialism. He wrote, "**if the cakes we eat were mere perceptions, they would not stop our hunger**".[36]

There are similar examples and some outrageous sentences such as "**you understand the existence of matter when you are slapped in the face**" in the books of famous materialists such as **Marx, Engels, Lenin**, and others.

The disorder in comprehension that gives way to these examples of the materialists is their interpreting the explanation of "matter is a perception" as "matter is a trick of light". They think that perception is limited to sight and that other faculties like touch have physical correlates. A bus knocking down a man makes them say "look, it crashed, therefore it is not a perception". They do not understand that all perceptions experienced during a bus crash, such as hardness, collision, and pain, are also formed in the brain.

## THE EXAMPLE OF DREAMS

The best example to explain this reality is the dream. A person can experience very realistic events in dream. He can roll down the stairs and break his leg, have a serious car accident, become stuck under a bus, or eat a cake and be satiated. Similar events to those experienced in our daily lives are also experienced in dreams with the same persuasive sense of their reality, and arousing the same feelings in us.

A person who dreams that he is knocked down by a bus can open his eyes in a hospital again in his dream and understand that he is disabled, but it is all a dream. He can also dream that he dies in a car crash, angels of death take his soul, and his life in the hereafter begins. (This latter event is experienced in the same manner in this life, which, just like the dream, is a perception.)

This person perceives very sharply the images, sounds, feelings of solidity, light, colours, and all other feelings pertaining to the event he experiences in his dream. The perceptions he perceives in his dream are as natural as the ones in "real" life. The cake he eats in his dream satiates him although it is a mere dream-sense perception, because being satiated is also a dream-sense perception. However, in reality, this person is lying in his bed at that moment. There are no stairs, traffic, or buses to consider. The dreaming person experiences and sees perceptions and feelings that do not exist in the external world. The fact that in our dreams, we experience, see, and feel events with no physical correlates in the "external world" very clearly reveals that the "external world" of our waking lives also consists absolutely of mere perceptions.

Those who believe in materialist philosophy, particularly **Marxists**, are enraged when they are told about this reality, the essence of matter. They quote examples from the superficial reasoning of **Marx**, **Engels**, or **Lenin** and make emotional declarations.

However, these persons must think that they can also make these declarations in their dreams. In their dreams, they can also read "*Das Kapital*", participate in meetings, fight with the police, be hit on the head, and feel the pain of their wounds. When asked in their dreams, they will think that

## THE WORLD IN DREAMS

For you, reality is all that can be touched with the hand and seen with the eye. In your dreams you can also "touch with your hand and see with your eye", but in reality, then you have neither hand nor eye, nor is there anything that can be touched or seen. There is no material reality that makes these things happen except your brain. You are simply being deceived.

What is it that separates real life and dreams from one another? Ultimately, both forms of living are brought into being within the brain. If we are able to live easily in an unreal world during our dreams, the same can equally be true for the world we live in while awake. When we wake up from a dream, there is no logical reason not to think that we have entered a longer dream called "real life". The reason we consider our dream a fancy and the world 'real' is only a product of our habits and prejudices. This suggests that we may well be awoken from the life on earth, which we think we are living right now, just as we are awoken from a dream.

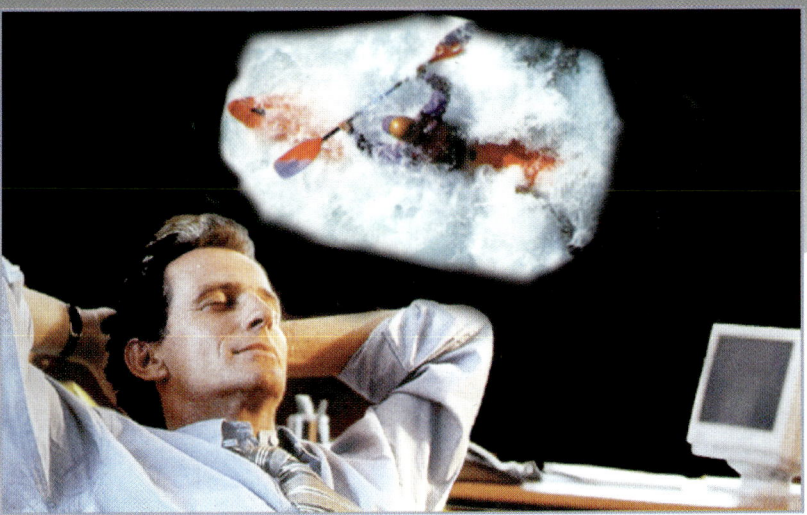

what they experience in their dreams also consists of "absolute matter", just as they assume the things they see when they are awake are "absolute matter". However, whether it is in their dreams or in their daily lives, all that they see, experience, or feel consists only of perceptions.

*A Very Different Approach to Matter*

## THE EXAMPLE OF CONNECTING THE NERVES IN PARALLEL

Let us consider the car crash example given by Politzer in which he talked of someone crushed by a car. If the crushed person's nerves travelling from his five senses to his brain, were connected to another person's, take Politzer's brain, with a parallel connection, at the moment the bus hit that person, it would also hit Politzer sitting at home at the same time. All the feelings experienced by that person having the accident would be experienced by Politzer, just like the same song listened to from two different loudspeakers connected to the same tape recorder. Politzer would feel, see, and experience the braking of the bus, the touch of the bus on his body, the images of a broken arm and blood, fractures, images of his entering the operation room, the hardness of the plaster cast, and the feebleness of his arm.

Every other person connected to the man's nerves in parallel would experience the accident from beginning to end just like Politzer. If the man in the accident fell into a coma, they would all fall into a coma. Moreover, if all the perceptions pertaining to the car accident were recorded in a device and if all these perceptions were transmitted to a person repeatedly, the bus would knock this person down many times.

So, which one of the buses hitting those people is real? The materialist philosophy has no consistent answer to this question. The right answer is that they all experience the car accident in all its details in their own minds.

The same principle applies to the cake and stone examples. If the nerves of the sense organs of Engels, who felt the satiety and fullness of the cake in his stomach after eating a cake, were connected to a second person's brain in parallel, that person would also feel full when Engels ate the cake and was satiated. If the nerves of Johnson, who felt pain in his foot when he delivered a sound kick to a stone, were connected to a second person in parallel, that person would feel the same pain.

So, which cake or which stone is the real one? The materialist philosophy again falls short of giving a consistent answer to this question. The correct and consistent answer is this: both Engels and the second person have eaten the cake in their minds and are satiated; both Johnson and the second person have fully experienced the moment of striking the stone in their minds.

Let us make a change in the example we gave about Politzer: let us connect the nerves of the man hit by the bus to Politzer's brain, and the nerves of Politzer sitting in his house to the brain of the man who is hit by the bus. In this case, Politzer will think that a bus has hit him although he is sitting in his house. The man actually hit by the bus will never feel the impact of the accident and think that he is sitting in Politzer's house. The very same logic may be applied to the cake and the stone examples.

As we see, it is not possible for man to transcend his senses and break free of them. In this respect, a man's soul can be exposed to all kinds of representations of physical events although it has no physical body and no material existence and lacks material weight. It is not possible for a person to realise this because he assumes these three-dimensional images to be real and is certain of their existence because, like everybody, he depends on perceptions experienced by his sensory organs.

The famous British philosopher David Hume expresses his thoughts on this fact:

> Frankly speaking, when I include myself in what I call "myself", I always come across with a specific perception pertaining to hot or cold, light or shadow, love or hatred, sour or sweet or some other notion. Without the existence of a perception, I can never capture myself in a particular time and **I can observe nothing but perception.**[37]

## THE FORMATION OF PERCEPTIONS IN THE BRAIN IS NOT PHILOSOPHY BUT SCIENTIFIC FACT

Materialists claim that what we have been saying here is a philosophical view. However, to hold that the "external world", as we call it, is a collection of perceptions is not a matter of philosophy but a plain scientific fact. How the image and feelings form in the brain is taught in medical schools in detail. These facts, proven by 20th-century science particularly physics, clearly show that matter does not have an absolute reality and that, in a sense, everyone is watching the "monitor in his brain".

Everyone who believes in science, be he an atheist, Buddhist, or someone who holds any other view, has to accept this fact. A materialist might deny the existence of a Creator yet he cannot deny this scientific reality.

The inability of Karl Marx, Friedrich Engels, Georges Politzer and others to comprehend such a simple and evident fact is still startling, although the level of scientific understanding of their times was perhaps insufficient. In our time, science and technology are highly advanced and recent discoveries make it easier to comprehend this fact. Materialists, on the other hand, are flooded with the fear of both comprehending this fact, even partially, and realising how definitely it demolishes their philosophy.

## THE GREAT FEAR OF THE MATERIALISTS

For a while, no substantial response came from materialist Turkish circles on the subject brought up in this book, that is, the fact that matter is a mere perception. This gave us the impression that our point had not been made so clear and that it needed further explanation. Yet, before long, it was revealed that materialists felt quite uneasy about the popularity of this subject, and felt a great fear of it.

For some time, materialists have been loudly proclaiming their fear and panic in their publications, conferences and panels. Their agitated and hopeless discourses imply that they are suffering a severe intellectual crisis. The scientific collapse of the theory of evolution, the so-called basis of their philosophy, had already come as a great shock to them. Now, they come to realise that they start to lose matter itself, which is a greater mainstay for them than Darwinism, and they are experiencing an even greater shock. They declare that this issue is the "biggest threat" to them and that it totally "demolishes their cultural fabric".

One of those who expressed most outspokenly the anxiety and panic felt by materialist circles was Renan Pekunlu, an academician as well as writer of the *Bilim ve Utopya* (Science and Utopia) periodical which has assumed the task of defending materialism. Both in his articles in *Bilim ve Utopya* and in the panels he attended, Pekunlu presented the book

*Evolution Deceit* by Harun Yahya as the number one "threat" to materialism. What disturbed Pekunlu even more than the chapters that invalidated Darwinism was the part you are currently reading. To his readers and audience, the latter of whom were only a handful, Pekunlu delivered the message, "do not let yourselves be carried away by the indoctrination of idealism and keep your faith in materialism". He quoted Vladimir I. Lenin, the leader of the bloody communist revolution in Russia, as reference. Advising everyone to read Lenin's century-old book titled *Materialism and Empirio-Criticism*, Pekunlu repeated the counsels of Lenin, "do not think over this issue, or you will lose track of materialism and be carried away by religion". In an article he wrote in the aforementioned periodical, he quoted the following lines from Lenin:

> Once you deny objective reality, given us in sensation, you have already lost every weapon against fideism, for you have slipped into agnosticism or subjectivism – and that is all that fideism requires. **A single claw ensnared, and the bird is lost.** And our Machists have all become ensnared in idealism, that is, in a diluted, subtle fideism; they became ensnared from the moment they took "sensation" not as an image of the external world but as a special "element". It is nobody's sensation, nobody's mind, nobody's spirit, nobody's will.[38]

These words clearly demonstrate that the fact which Lenin, in alarm, realised and wanted to take out both of his mind and the minds of his "comrades", also disturbs contemporary materialists in a similar way. However, Pekunlu and other materialists suffer a yet greater distress; because they are aware that this fact is now being put forward in a far more explicit, certain and convincing way than 100 years ago. It is for the first time in world history that this subject is being explained in such an irresistible way.

Nevertheless, the general picture is that a great number of materialist scientists still take a very superficial stand against the fact that "matter is

**Turkish materialist writer Rennan Pekunlu says that "the theory of evolution is not so important, the real threat is this subject", because he is aware that this subject nullifies matter, the only concept in which he has faith.**

*A Very Different Approach to Matter*

nothing but an illusion". The subject explained in this chapter is **one of the most important and most exciting subjects** that one can ever come across in one's life. There is no chance of them having faced such a crucial subject before. Still, the reactions of these scientists or the manner they employ in their speeches and articles hint at how shallow and superficial their comprehension is.

The reactions of some materialists to the subject discussed here show that their blind adherence to materialism has caused some kind of harm to their logic. For this reason, they are far removed from comprehending the subject. For instance, Alaattin Senel, also an academician and writer for *Bilim ve Utopya*, expressed similar sentiments as Rennan Pekunlu saying, **"Forget the collapse of Darwinism, the really threatening subject is this one"**. Sensing that his own philosophy has no basis, he made demands such as "prove what you say!" More interestingly, this writer has himself written lines revealing that he cannot grasp this fact, which he considers a menace.

For instance, in an article in which he discussed this subject exclusively, Senel accepts that the external world is perceived in the brain as an image. However, he then goes on to claim that images are divided into two: those having physical correlates and those that do not, and that images pertaining to the external world have physical correlates. In order to support his assertion, he gives "the example of the telephone". In summary, he wrote: "I do not know whether the images in my brain have correlates in the external world or not, but the same thing applies when I speak on the phone. When I speak on the telephone, I cannot see the person I am speaking to but I can have this conversation confirmed when I later see him face to face."39

By saying so, this writer actually means the following: "If we doubt our perceptions, we can look at the matter itself and check its reality." However, this is an evident misconception, because it is impossible for us to reach the matter itself. **We can never get out of our mind and know what is "outside".** Whether the voice on the telephone has a correlate or not can be confirmed by the person on the other end. However, this confirmation is also imagery, which is experienced in the mind.

These people also experience the same events in their dreams. For instance, Senel may also see in his dream that he speaks on the telephone and then have this conversation confirmed by the person to whom he spoke. Pekunlu may in his dream feel himself facing "a serious threat" and advising people to read century-old books of Lenin. However, no matter what they do, these materialists can never deny that the events they have experienced and the people they have talked to in their dreams are nothing but perceptions.

**Who, then, will confirm whether the images in the brain have correlates or not?** The shadow beings in the brain? Without doubt, it is impossible for materialists to find a source of information that can yield data concerning the outside of the brain and confirm it.

Conceding that all perceptions are formed in the brain, but assuming that one can step "out" of this and have the perceptions confirmed by the real external world, reveals that the intellectual capacity of the person is limited and that his reasoning is distorted.

However, any person with a normal level of understanding and reasoning can easily grasp these facts. Every unbiased person knows, in relation to all that we have said, that it is not possible for him to test the existence of the external world with his senses. Yet, it appears that blind adherence to materialism distorts the reasoning capacity of people. For this reason, contemporary materialists display severe logical flaws in their reasoning just like their mentors who tried to "prove" the existence of matter by kicking stones or eating cakes.

It also has to be said that this is not an astonishing situation, because inability to understand is a common trait of all unbelievers. In the Qur'an, Allah particularly states that they are **"a people without understanding"** (Surat al-Ma'idah: 58)

# MATERIALISTS HAVE FALLEN INTO THE BIGGEST TRAP IN HISTORY

The atmosphere of panic sweeping through materialist circles in Turkey, of which we have here mentioned only a few examples, shows that materialists face utter defeat, which they have never met before in history. That matter is simply a perception has been proven by modern science and it is put forward in a very clear, straightforward and forceful way. It only remains for materialists to see and acknowledge the collapse of the entire material world in which they blindly believe and on which they rely.

Materialist thought has always existed throughout the history of humanity. Being very assured of themselves and the philosophy they believe in, materialists revolted against Allah who created them. The scenario they formulated maintained that matter has no beginning or end, and that all these could not possibly have a Creator. Because of their arrogance, they denied Allah and took refuge in matter, which they held to have real existence. They were so confident in this philosophy that they thought that it would never be possible to put forth an explanation proving the contrary.

That is why the facts told in this book regarding the real nature of matter surprised these people so much. What has been told here destroyed the very basis of their philosophy and left no ground for further discussion. Matter, upon which they based all their thoughts, lives, their arrogance and denial, vanished all of a sudden. **How can materialism exist when matter does not?**

One of the attributes of Allah is His plotting against the unbelievers. This is stated in the verse "They plot and plan, and Allah too plans; but **Allah is the best of planners.**" (Surat al-Anfal: 30)

Allah entrapped materialists by making them assume that matter exists and, so doing, humiliated them in an unseen way. Materialists deemed their possessions, status, rank, the society to which they belong, the whole world and everything else to really exist and grew arrogant against Allah by relying on these. They revolted against Allah by being boastful and added to their unbelief. While so doing, they totally relied on matter. Yet, they are so lacking in understanding that they fail to think that Allah encompasses them round about. Allah announces the state to which the unbelievers are led as a result of their thick-headedness:

> Or do they intend a plot (against you)? But **those who defy Allah are themselves involved in a plot!** (Surat at-Tur: 52)

This is most probably their biggest defeat in history. While growing arrogant, materialists have been tricked and suffered a serious defeat in the war they waged against Allah by bringing up something monstrous against Him. The verse "Thus have We placed leaders in every town, its wicked men, to plot therein: but **they only plot against their own souls, and they perceive it not**" announces how unconscious these people who revolt against their Creator are, and how they will end up (Surat al- An'am: 123). In another verse the same fact is related as:

> Fain would they deceive Allah and those who believe, but **they only deceive themselves, and realise (it) not!** (Surat al-Baqarah: 2)

While the unbelievers try to plot, they do not realise a very important fact which is stressed by the words "they only deceive themselves, and realise (it) not!" in the verse. This is the fact that everything they experience is an imagination designed to be perceived by them, and all plots they devise are simply images formed in their brain just like every other act they perform. Their folly has made them forget that they are all alone with Allah and, hence, they are entrapped in their own devious plans.

No less than those unbelievers who lived in the past, those living today face a reality that will shatter their devious plans at their foundations. With the verse "**…feeble indeed is the cunning of Satan**" (Surat al-An'am: 76), Allah says that these plots were doomed to end in failure the day they were hatched. He gives good tidings to believers with the verse "**…not the least harm will their cunning do you.**" (Surat Ali 'Imran: 120)

In another verse Allah says: "But **the unbelievers, their deeds are like a mirage in sandy deserts,** which the man parched with thirst mistakes for water; until when he comes up to it, he finds it to be nothing." (Surat an-Nur: 39). Materialism, too, becomes a "mirage" for the rebellious just as it is stated in this verse; when they have recourse to it, they find it to be nothing but an illusion. Allah has deceived them with such a mirage, and beguiled them into perceiving this whole collection of images as real. All those "eminent" people, professors, astronomers, biologists, physicists, and all others regardless of their rank and post are simply deceived like children, and are humiliated because they took matter as their god. Assuming a collection of images to be absolute, they based their philosophy and ideology on it, became involved in serious discussions, and adopted so-called "intellectual" discourse. They deemed themselves wise enough to offer an argument about the truth of the universe and, more importantly, to dispute about Allah with their limited intelligence. Allah explains their situation in the following verse:

> **And (the unbelievers) plotted and planned, and Allah too planned,** and the best of planners is Allah. (Surat Ali 'Imran: 54)

It may be possible to escape from some plots; however, this plan of Allah against the unbelievers is so firm that there is no way of escape from it. No matter what they do or to whom they appeal, they can never find a helper other than Allah. As Allah informs in the Qur'an, **"they shall not find for them other than Allah a patron or a helper."** (Surat an-Nisa: 173)

Materialists never expected to fall into such a trap. Having all the means of the 20th century at their disposal, they thought they could grow obstinate in their denial and drag people to disbelief. Allah describes this everlasting mentality of unbelievers and their end as follows in the Qur'an:

> **They plotted and planned**, but **We too planned, even while they perceived it not.** Then see what was the end of their plot! This, that **We destroyed them and their people, all (of them)**. (Surat an-Naml: 50-51)

This, on another level, is what the verses come to mean: materialists are made to realise that everything they own is but an illusion, and therefore **everything they possess has been destroyed**. As they witness their possessions, factories, gold, dollars, children, spouses, friends, rank and status, and even their own bodies, all of which they deem to exist, slipping away from their hands, they are **"destroyed"** in the words of the 51st verse of Surat al-An'am. At this point, they are no more material entities but souls.

No doubt, realising this truth is the worst possible situation for materialists. The fact that everything they possess is only an illusion is tantamount, in their own words, to "death before dying" in this world.

This fact leaves them alone with Allah. With the verse, **"Leave Me alone, (to deal) with the (creature) whom I created (bare and) alone"**, Allah calls us to attend to the fact that each human being is, in truth, all alone in His presence. (Surat al- Muddaththir: 11). This remarkable fact is repeated in many other verses:

> And behold! You come to us **bare and alone** as We created you for the first time: you have left behind you all (the favours) which We bestowed on you... (Surat al-An'am: 6)
>
> And each one of them will come to Him on the Day of Resurrection, **alone**. (Surah Maryam: 19)

This, on another level, is what the verses indicate: those who take matter as their god have come from Allah and returned to Him. They have submitted their wills to Allah whether they want or not. Now they wait for the day of judgement when everyone of them will be called to account, however unwilling they may be to understand it.

## CONCLUSION

The subject we have explained so far is one of the greatest truths that you will ever be told in your lifetime. Proving that the whole material world is in reality a **"shadow being"**, this subject is the key to comprehending the being of Allah and His creation and of understanding that He is the only absolute being.

The person who understands this subject realises that the world is not the sort of place it is thought by most people to be. The world is not an absolute place with a true existence as supposed by those who wander aimlessly about the streets, get into fights in pubs, show off in luxurious cafes, brag about their property, or who dedicate their lives to hollow aims. The world is only a collection of perceptions, an illusion. All of the people we have cited above are only shadow beings who watch these perceptions in their minds; yet, they are not aware of this.

This concept is very important for it undermines the **materialist phi-**

**losophy** that denies the existence of Allah and causes it to collapse. This is the reason why materialists like **Marx**, **Engels**, and **Lenin** felt panic, became enraged, and warned their followers "not to think about" this concept when they were told about it. These people are so mentally deficient that they cannot even comprehend that perceptions are formed inside the brain. They assume that the world they watch in their brain is the "external world" and cannot comprehend obvious evidence to the contrary.

This unawareness is the outcome of the little wisdom Allah has given the disbelievers. As Allah says in the Qur'an, the unbelievers "**have hearts wherewith they understand not,** eyes wherewith they see not, and ears wherewith they hear not. They are like cattle – nay more misguided, for they are heedless (of warning)." (Surat al-A'raf: 179)

You can explore beyond this point by using the power of your personal reflection. For this, you have to concentrate, devote your attention, and ponder on the way you see the objects around you and the way you feel their touch. If you think heedfully, you can feel that the intelligent being that sees, hears, touches, thinks, and reads this book at this moment is only a soul and watches the perceptions called "matter" on a screen. The person who comprehends this is considered to have moved away from the domain of the material world that deceives a major part of humanity, and to have entered the domain of true existence.

This reality has been understood by a number of theists or philosophers throughout history. Islamic intellectuals such as Imam Rabbani, Muhyiddin Ibn al-'Arabi and Mawlana Jami realised this from the signs of the Qur'an and by using their reason. Some Western philosophers like George Berkeley have grasped the same reality through reason. Imam Rabbani wrote in his Maktubat (Letters) that the whole material universe is an "illusion and supposition (perception)" and that the only absolute being is Allah:

> Allah... The substance of these beings which He created is but nothingness... He created all in **the sphere of senses and illusions...** The existence of the universe is in the sphere of senses and illusions, and it is not material... In reality, there is nothing in the outside except the Glorious Being, (Who is Allah).[40]

Imam Rabbani explicitly stated that all images presented to man are only illusions, and that they have no originals in the "outside".

> This imaginary cycle is portrayed in imagination. It is seen to the extent that it is portrayed, yet, **with the mind's eye**. In the outside, it seems as if it is seen with the head's eye. However, the case is not so. It has neither a designation nor a trace in the outside. There is no circumstance to be seen. Even the face of a person reflected in a mirror is like that. It has no constancy in the outside. No doubt, both its constancy and image are in the **IMAGINATION.** Allah knows best.[41]

Mawlana Jami stated the same fact, which he discovered by following the signs of the Qur'an and by using his wit: **"Whatever there is in the universe are senses and illusions.** They are either like reflections in mirrors or shadows".

However, the number of those who have understood this fact throughout history has always been limited. Great scholars such as Imam Rabbani have written that it might not be wise to tell this fact to the masses because most people are not able to grasp it.

In the age in which we live, this has been made an empirical fact by the body of evidence put forward by science. The fact that the universe is a shadow being is described in such a concrete, clear, and explicit way for the first time in history.

For this reason, the **21st century will be a historical turning-point** when people will generally comprehend the divine realities and be led in crowds to Allah, the only Absolute Being. The materialistic creeds of the 19th century will be relegated to the trash-heaps of history, Allah's being and creating will be grasped, spacelessness and timelessness will be understood, humanity will break free of the centuries-old veils, deceits and superstitions confusing them.

It is not possible for this unavoidable course to be impeded by any shadow being.

# Relativity of Time and the Reality of Fate

Everything related so far demonstrates that "three-dimensional space" does not exist in reality, that it is a prejudice completely founded on perceptions and that one leads one's whole life in "spacelessness". To assert the contrary would be to hold a superstitious belief far removed from reason and scientific truth, for there is no valid proof of the existence of a three-dimensional material world.

This refutes the primary assumption of the materialist philosophy that underlies evolutionary theory, the assumption that matter is absolute and eternal. The second assumption upon which materialistic philosophy rests is the supposition that time is absolute and eternal. This is as superstitious as the first.

## THE PERCEPTION OF TIME

What we perceive as time is, in fact, a method by which one moment is compared to another. We can explain this with an example. For instance, when a person taps an object, he hears a particular sound. When he taps the same object five minutes later, he hears another sound. The person perceives that there is an interval between the first sound and the second and he calls this interval "time". Yet at the time he hears the second sound, the first sound he heard is no more than an imagination in his mind. It is merely a bit of information in his memory. The person formulates the concept of "time" by **comparing the moment in which he lives with what he has in his memory. If this comparison is not made, there can be no concept of time.**

Similarly, a person makes a comparison when he sees someone entering a room through a door and sitting in an armchair in the middle of the room. By the time this person sits in the armchair, the images related to the moments he opens the door, walks into the room, and makes his way to the armchair are compiled as bits of information in the brain. The perception of time occurs when one compares the man sitting in the armchair with those bits of information.

In brief, **time comes to exist as a result of the comparison made between some illusions stored in the brain.** If man did not have memory, then his brain would not make such interpretations and therefore would never have formed the concept of time. The only reason why someone determines himself to be thirty years old is because he has accumulated information pertaining to those thirty years in his mind. If his memory did not exist, then he would not think of the existence of such a preceding period and he would only experience the single "moment" in which he lives.

## THE SCIENTIFIC EXPLANATION OF TIMELESSNESS

Let us try to clarify the subject by quoting various scientists' and scholars' explanations of the subject. Regarding the subject of time flowing backwards, the famous intellectual and Nobel laureate professor of genetics, François Jacob, states the following in his book *Le Jeu des Possibles* (The Possible and the Actual):

> Films played backwards make it possible for us to imagine **a world in which time flows backwards**. A world in which milk separates itself from the coffee and jumps out of the cup to reach the milk-pan; a world in which light rays are emitted from the walls to be collected in a trap (gravity center) instead of gushing out from a light source; a world in which a stone slopes to the palm of a man by the astonishing cooperation of innumerable drops of water making the stone possible to jump out of water. Yet, in such a world in which time has such opposite features, **the processes of our brain and the way our memory compiles information, would similarly be functioning backwards.** The same is true for the past and future and the world will appear to us exactly as it currently appears.[42]

Since our brain is accustomed to a certain sequence of events, the world operates not as is related above and we assume that time always flows forward. However, this is a decision reached in the brain and is relative. In reality, we can never know how time flows or even whether it flows or not. This is an indication of the fact that **time is not an absolute fact but just a sort of perception.**

The relativity of time is a fact also verified by one of the most important physicists of the 20th century, Albert Einstein. Lincoln Barnett, writes in his book *The Universe and Dr. Einstein*:

> Along with absolute space, Einstein discarded the concept of absolute time – of a steady, unvarying inexorable universal time flow, streaming from the infinite past to the infinite future. Much of the obscurity that has surrounded the Theory of Relativity stems from man's reluctance to recognize that sense of **time, like sense of color, is a form of perception**. Just as space is simply a possible order of material objects, so **time is simply a possible order of events**. The subjectivity of time is best explained in Einstein's own words. "The experiences of an individual" he says, "appear to us arranged in a series of events; in this series **the single events which we remember appear to be ordered according to the criterion of 'earlier' and 'later'.** There exists, therefore, for the individual, an I-time, or **subjective time**. This in itself is not measurable. I can, indeed, associate numbers with the events, in such a way that a greater number is associated with the later event than with an earlier one.[43]

Einstein himself pointed out, as quoted in Barnett's book: "space and time are forms of intuition, which **can no more be divorced from consciousness** than can our concepts of colour, shape, or size." According to the Theory of General Relativity: **"time has no independent existence apart from the order of events by which we measure it."**[44]

Since time consists of perception, it depends entirely on the perceiver and is therefore relative.

The speed at which time flows differs according to the references we use to measure it because there is no natural clock in the human body to indicate precisely how fast time passes. As Lincoln Barnett wrote: "Just as there is no such thing as color without an eye to discern it, so an instant or an hour or a day is nothing without an event to mark it."[45]

The relativity of time is plainly experienced in dreams. Although what we see in our dreams seems to last for hours, in fact, it only lasts for a few minutes, and even a few seconds.

Let us think about an example to clarify the subject further. Let us assume that we were put in a room with a single window that was specifically designed and we were kept there for a certain period. Let there be a clock in the room from which we can see the amount of time that has passed. At the same time, let it be that we see from the window of the room the sun rising and setting at certain intervals. A few days later, the answer we would give to the question about the amount of time we spent in the room would be based both on the information we had collected by looking at the clock from time to time and on the computation we had made by referring to how many times the sun rose and set. For example, we estimate that we spent three days in the room. However, if the person who put us in that room said that we spent only two days in the room and that the sun we had seen from the window was produced artificially by a simulation machine and that the clock in the room was regulated specially to work faster, then the calculation we had done would have no meaning.

This example confirms that the information we have about the rate of passage of time is based on relative references. The relativity of time is a scientific fact also proven by scientific methodology. **Einstein's Theory of General Relativity** maintains that the speed of time changes depending on the speed of the object and its position in the gravitational field. As speed increases, time is shortened and compressed: it slows down as if coming to the point of "stopping".

Let us explain this with an example given by Einstein. Imagine two twins, one of whom stays on earth while the other goes travelling in space at a speed close to that of light. When he comes back, the traveller will see that his brother has grown much older than he has. The reason is that time flows much slower for the person who travels at speeds near the speed of light. Let us consider a space-travelling father and his earth-bound son. If the father were twenty-seven years old when he set out and his son three;

*Relativity of Time and the Reality of Fate*

when the father came back to earth thirty years later (earth time), the son would be thirty-three years old while his father would only be thirty.[46] This relativity of time is not caused by the deceleration or acceleration of clocks, or the deceleration of a mechanical spring. It is rather the result of the differentiated operation periods of the entire system of material existence, which goes as deep as sub-atomic particles. In other words, for the person experiencing it, the shortening of time is not experienced as if acting in a slow-motion picture. In such a setting where time shortens, one's heartbeats, cell replications, and brain functions, etc, all operate slower than those of the slower-moving person on earth. Nevertheless, the person goes on with his daily life and does not notice the shortening of time at all. Indeed the shortening does not even become apparent until comparison is made.

## RELATIVITY IN THE QUR'AN

The conclusion to which we are led by the findings of modern science is that **time is not an absolute fact as supposed by materialists, but only a relative perception.** What is most interesting is that this fact, undiscovered until the 20th century by science, was revealed to mankind in the Qur'an fourteen centuries ago. There are various references in the Qur'an to the relativity of time.

It is possible to see in many verses of the Qur'an the scientifically-proven fact that time is a psychological perception dependent on events, the setting, and conditions. For instance, a person's entire life is a very short time as we are informed in the Qur'an:

> On the Day when He will call you, and you will answer (His Call) with (words of) His Praise and Obedience, and you will think that you have stayed (in this world) **but a little while**! (Surat al-Isra: 52)
>
> And on the Day when He shall gather them together, (it will seem to them) as if they had not tarried (on earth) **longer than an hour of a day**: they will recognise each other. (Surah Yunus: 45)

Some verses indicate that people perceive time differently and that sometimes people can perceive a very short period as a very lengthy one. The following conversation of people held during their judgement in the hereafter is a good example of this:

> He will say: "What number of years did you stay on earth?" They will say: "We stayed **a day or part of a day**, but ask those who keep account." He will say: "You stayed not but a little, if you had only known!" (Surat al-Muminun: 112-114)

In some other verses Allah states that time may flow at different paces in different settings:

> Yet, they ask you to hasten on the punishment! But Allah will not fail in His promise. Verily **a day in the sight of your Lord is like a thousand years of your reckoning.** (Surat al-Hajj: 47)

> The angels and the spirit ascend unto Him in **a day the measure whereof is (as) fifty thousand years.** (Surat al-Ma'arij: 4)

> He rules (all) affairs from the heavens to the earth: in the end will (all affairs) ascend to Him in **a day the measure of which is a thousand years of what you count.** (Surat al-Sajda, 5)

These verses are clear expressions of the relativity of time. That this result, which was only recently understood by scientists in the 20th century, was communicated to man 1,400 years ago in the Qur'an is an indication of the revelation of the Qur'an by Allah, Who encompasses the whole of time and space.

Many other verses of the Qur'an reveal that time is a perception. This is particularly evident in the stories. For instance, Allah has kept the Companions of the Cave, a group of believing people mentioned in the Qur'an, in a deep sleep for more than three centuries. When they awoke, these people thought that they had stayed in that state but a little while, and could not reckon how long they had slept:

> Then We drew (a veil) over their ears, for a number of years, in the Cave, (so that they heard not). Then We raised them up that We might know which of the two parties would best calculate the time that they had tarried. (Surat al-Kahf: 11-12)

> Such (being their state), We raised them up (from sleep), that they might question each other. Said one of them, "How long have you stayed (here)?" They said, "We have stayed (perhaps) a day, or part of a day." (At length) they (all) said, "Allah (alone) knows best how long you have stayed here..." (Surat al-Kahf: 19)

The situation told in the verse below is also evidence that time is in truth a psychological perception.

> Or (take) the similitude of one who passed by a hamlet, all in ruins to its roofs. He said, "How shall Allah bring it (ever) to life, after (this) its death?" but Allah caused him to die for a hundred years, then raised him up (again). He said: "How long did you tarry (thus)?" He said: (Perhaps) a day or part of a day." He said: "Nay, you have tarried thus a hundred years; but look at your food and your drink; they show no signs of age; and look at your donkey. And that We may make of you a sign unto the people, look further at the bones, how We bring them together and clothe them with flesh." When this was shown clearly to him, he said: "I know that Allah has power over all things."

The above verse clearly emphasises that Allah, Who created time, is unbound by it. Man, on the other hand, is bound by time, which is ordained by Allah. As in the verse, man is even incapable of knowing how long he slept. In such a state, to assert that time is absolute (just as materialists, in their distorted thinking, do) is very unreasonable.

## DESTINY

This relativity of time clears up a very important matter. Relativity is so variable that a period appearing billions of years' duration to us may last only a second in another perspective. Moreover, an enormous period of time extending from the world's beginning to its end may not even last a second but just an instant in another dimension.

This is the very essence of the concept of destiny – a concept that is not well understood by most people, especially materialists who deny it completely. Destiny is Allah's perfect knowledge of all events past or future. A majority of people question how Allah can already know events that have not yet been experienced and this leads them to fail in understanding the authenticity of destiny. However, "events not yet experienced" are only so **for us**. Allah is not bound by time or space for He Himself has created them. For this reason, **past, future, and present are all the same to Allah; for Him everything has already taken place and finished.**

In *The Universe and Dr. Einstein*, Lincoln Barnett explains how the

Theory of General Relativity leads to this conclusion. According to Barnett, the universe can be **"encompassed in its entire majesty only by a cosmic intellect"**.[47] The will that Barnett calls "the cosmic intellect" is **the wisdom and knowledge of Allah, Who prevails over the entire universe.** Just as we can easily see a ruler's beginning, middle, and end, and all the units in between as a whole, Allah knows the time we are subject to as if it were a single moment right from its beginning to its end. People, however, experience incidents only when their time comes and they witness the destiny Allah has created for them.

It is also important to draw attention to the shallowness of the distorted understanding of destiny prevalent in our society. This distorted belief of fate is a superstition that Allah has determined a "destiny" for every man but that these destinies can sometimes be changed by people. For instance, people make superficial statements about a patient who returns from death's door such as "he defeated his destiny". No-one is able to change his destiny. The person who returned from death's door, didn't die precisely because he was destined not to die at that time. It is, ironically, the destiny of those people who deceive themselves by saying "I defeated my destiny" that they should say so and maintain such a mindset.

Destiny is the eternal knowledge of Allah and for Allah, Who knows time like a single moment and Who prevails over the whole of time and space; everything is determined and finished in destiny. We also understand from what He relates in the Qur'an that time is one for Allah: some incidents that appear to us to happen in the future are related in the Qur'an in such a way as if they had already taken place long before. For instance, the verses that describe the accounts that people must give to Allah in the hereafter are related as events which occurred long ago:

> And the trumpet **is blown**, and all who are in the heavens and all who are in the earth **swoon away**, save him whom Allah wills. Then it **is blown** a second time, and behold them standing waiting! And the earth **shone** with the light of her Lord, and the Book is set up, and the prophets and the witnesses **are brought**, and it **is judged** between them with truth, and they **are not wronged...** And those who disbelieve **are driven** unto hell in troops...: And those who feared their Lord **are driven** unto Paradise in troops" (Surat az-Zumar: 68-73)

Some other verses on this subject are:

> And every soul **came**, along with it a driver and a witness. (Surat al-Qaf: 21)
> And the heaven **is cloven asunder**, so that on that day it **is frail**. (Surat al-Haqqah: 16)
> And because they were patient and constant, He rewarded them with a garden and (garments of) silk. Reclining in the (garden) on raised thrones, they **saw** there neither the sun's (excessive heat) nor excessive cold. (Surat al-Insan: 12-13)
> And Hell **is placed** in full view for (all) to see. (Surat an-Nazi'at: 36)
> But on this day the believers **laugh** at the unbelievers (Surat al-Mutaffifin: 34)
> And the sinful **saw** the fire and **apprehended** that they have to fall therein: no means **did they find** to turn away therefrom. (Surat al-Kahf: 53)

As may be seen, occurrences that are going to take place after our death (from our point of view) are related in the Qur'an as past events already experienced. Allah is not bound by the relative time frame in which we are confined. Allah has willed these things in timelessness: people have already performed them and all these events have been lived through and are ended. He imparts in the verse below that every event, big or small, is within the knowledge of Allah and recorded in a book:

> In whatever business you may be, and whatever portion you may be reciting from the Qur'an, and whatever deed you (mankind) may be doing, We are witnesses thereof when you are deeply engrossed therein. Nor is hidden from your Lord (so much as) the weight of an atom on the earth or in heaven. And not the least and not the greatest of these things but are recorded in a clear record. (Surah Yunus: 61)

## THE WORRY OF THE MATERIALISTS

The issues discussed in this chapter, namely the truth underlying matter, timelessness, and spacelessness, are indeed extremely clear. As expressed before, these are definitely not any sort of philosophy or way of thought, but **scientific outcomes that are impossible to deny**. In addition to its being a technical reality, the evidence also admits of no other rational and logical alternatives on this issue: **the universe** is an **illusory entity** with all the matter composing it and all the creatures living in it. It is a collection of perceptions.

Materialists have a hard time understanding this issue. For instance, if we return to Politzer's bus example: although Politzer technically knew that he could not step out of his perceptions he could only admit it in certain cases. That is, for Politzer, events take place in the brain until the bus crash, but as soon as the bus crash takes place, things go out of the brain and gain a physical reality. The logical defect of this point is very clear. Politzer has made the same mistake as the materialist Johnson who said, "I hit the stone, my foot hurts, therefore it exists". Politzer could not understand that the shock felt after the impact of the bus was merely a perception as well.

The subliminal reason why materialists cannot comprehend this subject is their fear of what they will face when they comprehend it. Lincoln Barnett tells us that some scientists "discerned" this subject:

> Along with philosophers' reduction of all objective reality to a shadow-world of perceptions, scientists have become aware of the **alarming** limitations of man's senses.[48]

Any reference made to the fact that matter and time are perceptions arouses great fear in the materialist, because these are the only notions he relies on as absolute beings. He, in a sense, takes them as idols to worship; because he thinks that matter and time (through evolution) created him.

When he feels that the universe in which he thinks he is living, the world, his own body, other people, other materialist philosophers by whose ideas he is influenced, and, in short, everything is a perception, he feels overwhelmed by a horror at it all. Everything he depends on, believes in, and has recourse to suddenly vanishes. He feels a taste of the desperation which he will really experience on the day of judgement, as described in the verse "That day shall they (openly) show (their) submission to Allah; and **all their inventions left them in the lurch.**" (Surat an-Nahl: 87)

From then on, this materialist tries to convince himself of the reality of matter, and makes up "evidence" for this end. He hits his fist on the wall, kicks stones, shouts, yells, but can never escape from the reality.

*Relativity of Time and the Reality of Fate*

Just as they want to dismiss this reality from their minds, they also want other people to discard it. They are also aware that if people in general know the true nature of matter, the primitive nature of their own philosophy and the ignorance of their worldview will be bared for all to see, and there will be no ground left on which they can found their views. These fears are the reasons why they are so disturbed at the facts related here.

Allah states that the fears of the unbelievers will be intensified in the hereafter. On the day of judgement, they will be addressed thus:

> One day shall We gather them all together. We shall say to those who ascribed partners (to Us): **"Where are the partners whom you (invented and) talked about?"** (Surat al-An'am: 22)

After that, unbelievers will witness their possessions, children and their intimates, whom they had assumed to be real and had ascribed as partners to Allah, leaving them and vanishing. Allah informs us of this in the verse **"Behold! How they lie against their own selves! But the (lie) which they invented left them in the lurch."** (Surat al-An'am: 24).

## THE GAIN OF BELIEVERS

While the fact that matter and time are perceptions alarms materialists, the opposite holds true for believers. People of faith become very glad when they perceive the secret behind matter, because this reality is the key to all questions. With this key, all secrets are unlocked. One comes easily to understand many issues that one previously had difficulty in understanding.

As said before, the questions of death, paradise, hell, the hereafter, changing dimensions, and questions such as "Where is Allah?" "What was before Allah?" "Who created Allah?" "How long will life in the grave last?" "Where are heaven and hell?" and "Where do heaven and hell currently exist?" are easily answered. It will be understood with what kind of order Allah created the entire universe from out of nothing, so much so that, with this secret, **the questions of "when?" and "where?" become meaningless** because there are no time and no space left. When spacelessness is grasped, it will be understood that hell, heaven and earth are all actually

**the same place**. If timelessness is grasped, it will be understood that everything takes place at **a single moment**: nothing is waited for and time does not go by, because everything has already happened and finished.

With this secret delved, **the world becomes like heaven for a believer.** All distressful material worries, anxieties, and fears vanish. The person grasps that the entire universe has a single sovereign, that He changes the entire physical world as He pleases and that all one has to do is to turn to Him. He then submits himself entirely to Allah "**to be devoted to His service**". (Surat Ali 'Imran: 35)

To comprehend this secret is the greatest gain in the world.

With this secret, another very important reality mentioned in the Qur'an is unveiled: that "**Allah is nearer to man than his jugular vein**" (Surah Qaf: 16). As everybody knows, the jugular vein is inside the body. What could be nearer to a person than his inside? This situation can easily be explained by the reality of spacelessness. This verse also can be much better comprehended by understanding this secret.

This is the plain truth. It should be well established that there is no helper and provider for man other than Allah. **There is nothing but Allah;** He is the only absolute being with Whom one can seek refuge, to Whom one can appeal for help and count on for reward.

Wherever we turn, there is the presence of Allah.

# Conclusion

Unquestionably, nothing can be more important than the creation of man and his knowing his Creator. What we have done throughout the book is to try to comprehend a subject that is an issue of the utmost importance for every person.

We think it necessary to remind the reader at this point that one does not need reams of information to grasp that the universe and everything in it, including oneself, have been created. It is as much within the scope of the conscience and reason of a small child as it is within that of an adult to grasp that he was created. The prophet Ibrahim's words in the Qur'an are a very good example of what we mean.

The Prophet Ibrahim once lived in a community that did not believe in Allah and worshipped totem poles instead. Although he had never received any teaching about the existence of Allah, he had grasped with his reason and conscience that he had been created–moreover, that he had been created by Allah, Who created the heavens and the earth. In the Qur'an it is related like this:

> When the night covered him over, he saw a star. He said: "This is my Lord." But when it set, he said: "I love not those that set." When he saw the moon rising in splendour, he said: "This is my Lord." But when the moon set, he said: "Unless my Lord guides me, I shall surely be among those who go astray." When he saw the sun rising in splendour, he said: "This is my Lord; this is the greatest (of all)." But when the sun set, he said: "O my people! I am indeed free from your (guilt) of giving partners to Allah. For me, I have set my face, firmly and truly, towards Him Who created the heavens and the earth, and never shall I ascribe partners to Allah." (Surat al-Anaam, 76-79)

As we see in the example of the Prophet Ibrahim, everyone who has reason and conscience and, more importantly, who "does not reject in iniquity and arrogance" is capable of understanding that the universe was created and, moreover, that it was created with a great order and plan.

No doubt the state of those who reject the existence of Allah, despite all the manifest signs displayed for all to see, is quite astonishing to those who have reason and conscience. In the Qur'an, the following is stated about those who do not believe in Allah's power of creation:

> If you marvel (at their want of faith), strange is their saying: "When we are (actually) dust, shall we indeed then be in a creation renewed?" They are those who deny their Lord! They are those round whose necks will be yokes (of servitude): they will be companions of the fire, to dwell therein (for aye)! (Surat al-Rad, 5)

The things related in this book are more important than anything else in your life. Perhaps you have so far failed to give due consideration to the importance of this subject or perhaps you may never have even thought about it before. However, be assured that to recognise Allah, Who has created you, is more important and urgent than anything else you can do.

Think about what He has granted you: you live in a world subtly-planned down to its slightest detail and created specially for you. You had no part in this process. You opened your eyes one day and found yourself amidst countless blessings. You can see, you can hear, you can feel…

And it is so because He willed such a creation. In a verse it is said:

> It is He Who brought you forth from the wombs of your mothers when you knew nothing; and He gave you hearing and sight and intelligence and affections: that you may give thanks (to Allah). (Surat an-Nahl, 78)

As stated in the verse, it is none but Allah Who has given you everything you own and Who created the universe you live in. Therefore, come and submit your whole self to Allah and be grateful to Him for all the blessings He has endowed you with and thereby earn an eternal reward. If you do the opposite, you will be showing ingratitude and exposing yourself to a penalty that, by the will of Allah, shall last forever.

Be assured: He does exist and He is very close to you…

He sees and knows everything that you do, and hears every word you utter…

And be assured that everyone, including you, will soon give account to Him…

Glory to You, of knowledge we have none, save what You have taught us: In truth it is You Who are perfect in knowledge and wisdom.
(Surat al-Baqara, 32)

# FOOTNOTES

## PART I: THE FACT OF CREATION IN THE LIGHT OF SCIENTIFIC EVIDENCE

1. George Politzer, *Principes Fondamentaux de Philosophie*, Editions Sociales, Paris, 1954, p. 84
2. Recounted in Jaki, S. (1980) Cosmos and Creator Regnery Gateway, Chicago
3. Stephen Hawking, *Evreni Kucaklayan Karinca*, Alkim Kitapcilik ve Yayincilik, 1993, p. 62-63
4. Henry Margenau and Roy Abraham Varghese, eds., Cosmos, Bios, Theos, La Salle, IL: Open Court Publishing, 1992, p. 241
5. Hugh Ross, Ph.D., *The Creator and the Cosmos*, Navpress, 1995, p. 76
6. W.R. Bird, *The Origin of Species Revisited*, Nashville: Thomas Nelson, 1991; originally published by Philosophical Library in 1987, p. 462
7. W.R. Bird, *The Origin of Species Revisited*, Nashville: Thomas Nelson, 1991; originally published by Philosophical Library in 1987, pp. 405-406
8. Stephen W. Hawking, *A Brief History of Time*, Bantam Books, April, 1988, p. 121
9. Paul Davies, *God and the New Physics*, New York: Simon & Schuster, 1983, p. 189
10. Hugh Ross, *The Fingerpring of God*, 2nd. Ed., Orange, CA: Promise Publishing Co., 1991, pp. 114-115
11. A Dorling Kindersley Book – *The Science*, published in the United States by Dorling Kindersley Inc., p. 24
12. Stephen Hawking, *Evreni Kucaklayan Karinca*, Alkim Kitapcilik ve Yayincilik, 1993, p. 143
13. *Bilim ve Teknik* magazine, vol. 203, p. 25
14. *Larousse Dictionary and Encyclopaedia*, Vol. II, p. 5734
15. Maurice Burton, C.B.P.C. Publishing Limited, *Encyclopaedia of Animals*, Reptiles, p. 120
16. Ibid, p. 120
17. Michael J. Behe, *Darwin's Black Box*, New York: Free Press, 1996, p. 232-233
18. Grzimeks Tierleben Vögel 3, Deutscher Taschen Buch Verlag, Oktober 1993, p. 92
19. Ibid, p. 89
20. Ibid, p. 87-88
21. David Attenborough, *The Private Life of Plants*, Princeton University Press, 1995, p. 291
22. *Nature*, 12 November, 1981
23. Michael Baigent, Richard Leigh, Henry Lincoln, *The Messianic Legacy*, Gorgi Books, London: 1991, p. 177-178.
24. D.M.S. Watson, "Adaptation", *Nature*, no. 124, p. 233
25. Richard Levontin, *The Demon-Haunted World*, The New York Review of Books, January, 9, 1997, p. 28
26. J. De Vries, *Essential of Physical Science*, Wm.B.Eerdmans Pub.Co., Grand Rapids, SD 1958, p. 15.
27. Timothy R. Stout, Tim Stout's Creation-Science Page.
28. Ibid.
29. Umit Simsek, *Big Bang: Kainatin Dogusu* (Big Bang: The Birth of the Universe), p. 55
30. David Darling, *Deep Time*, Delacorte Press, 1989, New York.
31. Robert Matthews, *Unravelling the Minde of God*, London Bridge, July, 1995, p.8
32. *Bilim ve Teknik*, June 1997, p. 60

## PART II: THOSE WHO ARE UNABLE TO SEE THE FACT OF CREATION

1. Charles Darwin, *The Origin of Species: By Means of Natural Selection or the Preservation of Favoured Races in the Struggle for Life*, London: Senate Press, 1995, p. 134.
2. Derek A. Ager. "The Nature of the Fossil Record." *Proceedings of the British Geological Association*, vol. 87, no. 2, (1976), p. 133.
3. T.N. George, "Fossils in Evolutionary Perspective", *Science Progress*, vol.48, (January 1960), p.1-3
4. Richard Monestarsky, Mysteries of the Orient, *Discover*, April 1993, p.40.
5. Stefan Bengston, *Nature* 345:765 (1990).
6. Earnest A. Hooton, *Up From The Ape*, New York: McMillan, 1931, p.332.
7. Stephen Jay Gould, Smith Woodward's Folly, *New Scientist*, 5 April, 1979, p. 44.
8. Charles E. Oxnard, The Place of Australopithecines in Human Evolution: Grounds for Doubt, *Nature*, No. 258, p. 389.
9. Richard Leakey, *The Making of Mankind*, London: Sphere Books, 1981, p. 116
10. Eric Trinkaus, Hard Times Among the Neanderthals, *Natural History*, No. 87, December 1978, p. 10, R.L. Holoway, "The Neanderthal Brain: What was Primitive?", *American Journal of Physical Anthrophology Supplement*, No. 12, 1991, p. 94

*Footnotes*

11. Ali Demirsoy, *Kalitim ve Evrim* (Inheritance and Evolution), Ankara: Meteksan Yayinlari 1984, p. 61
12. Ali Demirsoy, *Kalitim ve Evrim* (Inheritance and Evolution), Ankara: Meteksan Yayinlari 1984, p. 61
13. *Fabbri Britannica Science Encyclopaedia*, Vol. 2, No. 22, p. 519
14. Kevin McKean, *Bilim ve Teknik*, No. 189, p. 7
15. Frank B. Salisbury, "Doubts about the Modern Synthetic Theory of Evolution", *American Biology Teacher*, September 1971, p. 336.
16. Ali Demirsoy, *Kalitim ve Evrim* (Inheritance and Evolution), Ankara: Meteksan Publishing Co., 1984, p. 39.
17. Homer Jacobson, "Information, Reproduction and the Origin of Life", *American Scientist*, January, 1955, p.121.
18. Reinhard Junker & Siegfried Scherer, "Entstehung Gesiche Der Lebewesen", Weyel, 1986, p. 89.
19. Michael J. Behe, *Darwin's Black Box*, New York: Free Press, 1996, pp. 232-233.
20. C. L., Opposition to Freemasonry (Mason Aleyhtarligi), *Mimar Sinan*, Year 4, No 13, 1973, pp. 87-88.
21. Dr. Selami Isindag, "Obstacles to the Flourishing of Wisdom and Freemasonry", *Mason Dergisi* (Mason Magazine), Year: 24, Volume:25-26 (December, 76-March, 77).
22. *Mimar Sinan* magazine, volume 6, p. 66.
23. *Mason Dergisi* (Mason Magazine), volume 23-24, p. 41, 1976.
24. Michael Howard, *The Occult Conspiracy: The Secret History of Mystics*, Templars, Masons and Occult Societies, 1.b., London: Rider, 1989, p.63
25. Frederick Vester, *Denken, Lernen, Vergessen*, vga, 1978, p.6
26. George Politzer, *Principes Fondamentaux de Philosophie*, Editions Sociales, Paris, 1954, pp.38-39-44
27. R.L.Gregory, *Eye and Brain: The Psychology of Seeing*, Oxford University Press Inc., New York, 1990, p.9
28. Lincoln Barnett, *The Universe and Dr.Einstein*, William Sloane Associate, New York, 1948, p.20
29. Orhan Hançerlioglu, *Düsünce Tarihi (The History of Thought)*, Istanbul: Remzi Bookstore, 6.ed., September, 1995, p.447
30. V.I.Lenin, *Materialism and Empirio-criticism*, Progress Publishers, Moscow, 1970, p.14
31. Bertrand Russell, *ABC of Relativity*, George Allen and Unwin, London, 1964, pp.161-162
32. R.L.Gregory, *Eye and Brain: The Psychology of Seeing*, Oxford University Press Inc. New York, 1990, p.9
33. Karl Pribram, David Bohm, Marilyn Ferguson, Fritjof Capra, *Holografik Evren 1(Holographic Universe 1)*, translated by Ali Çakiroglu, Kuraldisi Publishing, Istanbul: 1996, p37
34. George Politzer, *Principes Fondamentaux de Philosophie*, Editions Sociales, Paris 1954, p.53
35. Orhan Hançerlioglu, *Düsünce Tarihi (The History of Thought)*, Istanbul: Remzi Bookstore, 6.ed., September, 1995, p.261
36. George Politzer, *Principes Fondamentaux de Philosophie*, Editions Sociales, Paris 1954, p.65
37. Paul Davies, *Tanri ve Yeni Fizik, (God and The New Physics)*, translated by Murat Temelli, Im Publishing, Istanbul 1995, pp.180-181
38. Rennan Pekünlü, "Aldatmacanin Evrimsizligi", (Non-Evolution of Deceit) *Bilim ve Ütopya*, December, 1998, (V.I.Lenin, Materialism and Empirio-criticism, Progress Publishers, Moscow, 1970, pp.334-335)
39. Alaettin Senel, "Evrim Aldatmacasi mi?, Devrin Aldatmacasi mi?", (Evolution Deceit or Deceit of the Epoch?) *Bilim ve Ütopya*, December 1998
40. *Imam Rabbani Hz. Mektuplari* (Letters of Rabbani), Vol.II, 357. Letter, p.163
41. *Imam Rabbani Hz. Mektuplari* (Letters of Rabbani), Vol.II, 470. Letter, p.1432
42. François Jacob, *Le Jeu des Possibles*, University of Washington Press, 1982, p.111
43. Lincoln Barnett, *The Universe and Dr.Einstein*, William Sloane Associate, New York, 1948, pp. 52-53
44. Lincoln Barnett, *The Universe and Dr.Einstein*, William Sloane Associate, New York, 1948, p.17
45. Lincoln Barnett, *The Universe and Dr.Einstein*, William Sloane Associate, New York, 1948, p.58.
46. Paul Strathern, *The Big Idea: Einstein and Relativity*, Arrow Books, 1997, p. 57
47. Lincoln Barnett, *The Universe and Dr.Einstein*, William Sloane Associate, New York, 1948, p.84
48. Lincoln Barnett, *The Universe and Dr.Einstein*, William Sloane Associate, New York, 1948, pp.17-18